Florida Place Names of Indian Origin and Seminole Personal Names

Florida Place Names of Indian Origin and Seminole Personal Names

WILLIAM A. READ

With an Introduction by
PATRICIA RILES WICKMAN

THE UNIVERSITY OF ALABAMA PRESS
Tuscaloosa

To
My friend and colleague
Hoguet A. Major

Copyright © 2004
The University of Alabama Press
Tuscaloosa, Alabama 35487-0380
All rights reserved
Manufactured in the United States of America

Originally published by Louisiana State University Press, 1934

∞
The paper on which this book is printed meets the minimum requirements of
American National Standard for Information Science–Permanence of Paper for
Printed Library Materials, ANSI Z39.48-1984.

Library of Congress Cataloging-in-Publication Data

Read, William Alexander, 1869–1962.
Florida place names of Indian origin and Seminole personal
names / William A. Read.
p. cm.
Originally published: Baton Rouge : Louisiana State University Press, 1934.
Includes bibliographical references and index.
ISBN 0-8173-5071-3 (pbk. : alk. paper)
1. Names, Geographical—Florida. 2. Names, Indian—Florida.
3. Names, Seminole. I. Title.
F309 .R32 2004
917.59'001'4—dc21   2003012352

CONTENTS

INTRODUCTION TO THE 2003 EDITION
Patricia Riles Wickman

The first native peoples of what is now the United States to meet and interact with Europeans on a long-range basis were the peoples of the lower Southeast. Their naming systems were flexible and fluid. They had no global imaging of themselves. They were—individual isolates and a few controversies aside—elements of the larger Maskókî linguistic family that covered almost all of present-day Florida, Georgia, South Carolina, Alabama, Mississippi, and eastern portions of Louisiana, Tennessee, and Kentucky. Nineteenth-century English speakers have transliterated this designator as "Muscogee"—a spelling that barely conveys the sound of the spoken word.

We shall never know with any certainty how many dialects derived from this mother tongue and from the social template that contained an orderly system for the genesis of new villages and the growth of towns and cities, all of which are based on an inherent dynamism that has been consistently underestimated ever since the Spaniards led the boat parade of European colonialization. It is always risky to characterize culture through linguistics; nevertheless, language mirrors and symbolizes culture—a fact that must be seriously considered in any attempt to use hindsight to image a culture.

We non-natives see poorly the people whom we have imaged only for the last couple of centuries as *Seminolies* or *Seminoles*. There are sixteen federally recognized tribes (known today as "FR tribes") that descend from the southeastern clans and tribes, which may be referred to generically as the Maskókî peoples. Of these, slightly more than half retain one or more of the names they were using when the Spaniards arrived. The rest reflect the natural evolution that would have taken place irrespective of various European transliterations, together with historical processes that have acted upon them over the last half millennium as a result of the European presence. Nevertheless, under no circumstances should we continue today to view these people as victims of historical processes. Their survival—their presence to this day--gives the lie to that cultural chauvinism. Their culture is alive, viable, and still dynamic; otherwise, how would they continue to exist as discrete social groups?

Many of their dialects continue to this day—each functioning as a distinct language after more than 500 years of both natural and artificial centrifugal forces have separated the speakers geographically. Maskókî, the linguistic mother, has been known since the early eighteenth century by the English-applied misnomer of "Creek." It still functions in both Florida and Oklahoma, and Maskókî speakers in each group understand one another fairly well.

A dialect known in the seventeenth and eighteenth centuries as *Hitchiti* (pronounced ITCH it eeh) continues today as *Mikí:suukî* (Miccosukee, Mikisuki), although we may never know whether its current name is the result of an internal, orderly, evolutionary process of cultural mitosis or whether it is yet another external cultural misunderstanding. We do not even know whether Mikí:suukî itself is a phrase in the core language, Maskókî, or a phrase in the Hitchiti dialect. The two remain so close in many instances that at times it is extremely difficult to untangle them, and the lack of understanding (and interest) on the part of European and Euroamerican reporters has only exacerbated the linguistic entanglement.

If the phrase (and it is a phrase, not a single word) had its genesis in core Maskókî, then it is a combination of *mikkó* (a civic and honorific title, literally, 'a keeper', known today by English speakers as *micco* and mistranslated variously as 'chief', 'king', or 'governor'), and *suukí* (literally, "a lot of them"). If the phrase arose in Hitchiti, however, it derives from *mikkí(t)* (the Hitchiti equivalent of mikkó, also a social position, a keeper, but used here in an additional, economic sense), and *suúki* (pigs)—in other words, "the leader of a town rich in livestock." The social systems of the people who used the phrase seem to support the latter, rather than the former, interpretation because it would have been inappropriate for a town—even one rich in livestock—to have supported multiple civic leaders.

Mikí:suukî survives solely in Florida, as the dominant language among the citizens of the Seminole Tribe of Florida and the Miccosukee Tribe of Indians of Florida (the only remaining FR tribes in Florida). At some undetermined point prior to the eighteenth century, and probably prior to the sixteenth century, core Maskókî and Hitchiti separated sufficiently to become mutually exclusive languages. Today speakers of one language in Florida cannot understand the other, although the linguistic ties that have bound the two historically are eminently clear to speakers of each. For example, Maskókî *ichó* (deer) is *ichî* in Mikí:suukî, and *ifá* (dog) is *ifî*. There are many more.

There are individual Mikí:suukî word survivals among the removed kin in Oklahoma, the citizens of the Seminole Nation of Oklahoma, where such survivals are referred to as "old language" and have been subsumed by the dominant Maskókî language. According to a consensus of opinions, the last fluent Mikí:suukî speaker among the Oklahoma Seminoles died within the last decade. The resulting mix of old Hitchiti/Mikí:suukî and core Maskókî (Creek) sometimes is referred to as "Seminole" by its Western speakers, although apparently there never has been a distinct "Seminole" language. Further, the proportion of Hitchiti/Mikí:suukî survivals in the mix appears to be very small and dwindling.

Concerning the use of the designator "Seminole" as a language and as synonymous with core Maskókî, Read seems to have been misled—possibly by John R. Swanton and by the fact that the modern subsumption process of Hitchiti/Mikí:suukî into core Maskókî in Oklahoma was taking place even as Swanton was working there. Removed (Oklahoma) Seminoles speak fluently only to Maskókî speakers among the Florida Seminole and Miccosukee tribes, although the Oklahoma accents have changed appreciably in relation to more than a century of direct contact with English speakers, compared to less than half a century in Florida.

Inherent in the use of "Seminole" as synonymous with Maskókî is a danger that presents the largest obstacle to the use of the present work. Creating a Seminole language and equating it with Maskókî leaves the reader with the erroneous impression that the majority of Florida's Indians were, and are, core Maskókî speakers. In turn, this tends to support the traditionalist imaging of today's Florida Indians as "Creeks" who moved into Florida from Georgia and Alabama—relative newcomers with little or no cultural and historical equity in Florida.

Such was not and is not the case. Although Maskókî has proven to be the more durable language among the removed Seminoles and Creeks in Oklahoma, it remains the subordinate language among the original descendents still in place in Florida. Here, virtually all of the citizens of the Miccosukee tribe and approximately three-fourths of the citizens of the Seminole tribe are first-language Mikí:suukî speakers. Through intermarriages and clan-camp amalgamations that have taken place over the last two hundred years (at least), and particularly as a result of the vicissitudes of the nineteenth-century Wars of Removal, there is a significant percentage of citizens of both Florida tribes who can speak, or at least understand, both languages. This is especially the case among the oldest third of both tribes, who speak almost no English.

Read does appear to appreciate the linguistic affinity between Mikí:suukî and Choctaw, a Western Maskókî dialect. Mikí:suukî speakers today comment frequently on the affinity of the two languages, and laugh together over the relative ease with which they understand one another. This affinity may be the source of Read's belief that some Florida place names are Choctaw in origin, when they could just as well be, with more historical probability, Mikí:suukî.

In addition, borrowed words from Spanish survive in both languages. This is to be expected because the Spaniards were not only the first to meet the ancestors of the Florida Indians but were also their neighbors (positive or negative) for the longest duration.

It will be the year 2056 before Florida will have been a part of the United States for as long as it was a part of the seaborne empire of Spain, and it will be 3006 if we include the half century of intermittent contacts during the *Entrada* period.

Examples of borrowed words from Spanish include the Mikí:suukî *cawayî* for 'horse', from the Spanish *caballo*, which has augmented but never replaced the old term *ichî chobî*, or 'big deer'. From the Spanish *capitán* or 'captain', the Miki:suuki speakers have derived *capitani* and the Maskókî speakers alter the pronunciation only slightly, to *cubidani*, both of which are understood as 'boss.' In Maskókî, *waka*, or 'cow', clearly derives from the Spanish *vaca*, and *mulato* seems to have been taken into the language directly without a change in pronunciation. There are a number of others, and the people themselves recall the origin of these words and their long associations with the Spaniards. Interestingly, their memories of associations with the Spaniards are imaged as positive—both in Florida and in Oklahoma—perhaps in historical opposition to the more recent, and all too frequently negative, imagings of their relations with the Euroamericans.

Uchî (Uchee, Euchee, Yuchi) is still used in ceremonial dance chants ("songs") at the Euchee dance ground in Oklahoma, and *Yamáshî* (Yamasee; Maskókî, "they have been tamed; we have conquered them") words survive in Oklahoma also. The last direct Yamáshî descendent in Florida died only in the 1990s. The last speakers of the dialect used by the *Calushathî(t)* (in Mikí:suukî; *Calusálki* in Maskókî) people, who are indicated as *Calusa* by the Spaniards, may have survived into the twentieth century, but this is not certain. When Frances Densmore—a musicologist working under the auspices of the Smithsonian Institution, Bureau of American Ethnology—recorded songs in South Florida during the 1930s, she was offered *Calushathî(t)* songs that may well have been within the living memory of the singers.

All of this discussion underscores the fact that following linguistic lineage is sometimes as messy as pursuing genetic lineage, and for many of the same reasons. But the vitality of the core language and at least one of its dialects remain, but some of its other dialects are dying quickly. For this reason, among others, the current reprint of William A. Read's linguistic examination of *Florida Place-Names of Indian Origin and Seminole Personal Names* will be valuable to future generations of humanities scholars, as well as to the interested general public.

William Alexander Read (1869–1962), was a native of Virginia. As a student of English, he acquired impressive academic credentials in Germanic and Romance philology in the United States, Europe, and England. Most of his professional life, thirty-eight years, was spent at Louisiana State University in Baton Rouge, where he served as head of the English Department and retired from that institution in 1940, six years after publishing his Florida work. Three years after the release of the Florida book, Read published *Indian Place Names in Alabama* (1937; reprint, Tuscaloosa: University of Alabama Press, 1984). A third and also correlative work, focusing on Georgia, was never completed, and remains in fragmentary manuscript form. Professor Read did not visit Florida while he was compiling his *Florida Place-Names of Indian Origin and Seminole Personal Names*, contenting himself, as he admits, with consulting US Postal Officials and other non-native sources for information on words about which he could not make his own decisions, "without [otherwise] incurring the expense of a trip through Florida." Ironically, he died in Miami, Florida, in 1962, finally in a position to hear the languages he had examined from a cultural and linguistic distance spoken in their original context. One wonders whether he might have revisited any of his earlier conclusions as a result.

He turned his attention numerous times to the Maskókî language family of the Southeast, choosing to segregate his studies in accordance with modern, impositional, state lines. Nevertheless, he understood to a great extent the relationships among the sisters and aunts in this linguistic family. Nevertheless, he lacked an understanding of the profound degree of subtlety that distinguishes the members of the family—an understanding that could have been acquired only by practical experience.

David Jumper (1946–) recalls being told by Josie Billie (1887–1980), a powerful and controversial medicine man, that there were still twelve languages in currency when he (Josie) was growing up. The figure twelve may or may not be precise, but the point remains: Mikí:suukî and Maskókî speakers have come to dominate the linguistic spectrum only during the most recent times. This certainly accords with the memories indicated above concerning the passing of Yamáshî, Uchî, and, possibly, Calushathî(t) speakers during the twentieth century. Incidentally, it again reaffirms the vitality of the Maskókî linguistic family and, perforce, of the people themselves.

There is acknowledgment, among the speakers of both languages, that the medicine songs (i.e., the ritual chants that infuse the herbal medicines with power) are all recalled and passed down to succeeding generations in what is referred to simply as "old language." It may be inferred by this that "old language" is an antiquated form of Maskókî that may be descended from the core language, or may be descended through a now-extinct dialect, other than Mikí:suukî. It is true that modern speakers of core Maskókî have less difficulty in understanding the songs than do modern Mikí:suukî speakers, but many words remain obscure to both.

A positive element of Read's never having visited Florida during his research is that, by involving postmasters and other non-native settlers "on the scene" in the state's small towns, Read was able to access local reminiscences that may explain formerly unexplainable (i.e., untranslatable) or "artificial" names. (See, for example, his explanation of "Wimauma" in his introduction.) It is a source of constant amusement to the Florida Seminoles to discover the ways in which English speakers have heard the Mikí:suukî and Maskókî words and rendered them into barely recognizable, or completely unrecognizable, words whose only remaining value is that they may be accommodated by the English pronunciation system. Many such confusions may never be straightened out completely.

The following two points are illustrative of such confusion. In his work on Alabama, Read translates "Boguechitto" as "Big Creek," accepting it as a Choctaw phrase composed of *bok* or 'creek', and *chito*, 'big' (p. 8). It is just as likely, however, given the geographic location of the site and its occupational history, that the phrase actually is "a place where snakes live" from the

core Maskókî, *chitto* or 'snake', and *abókita* for "they live there."
Among Florida place names, the same core Maskókî root from
which *abókita* derives also appears as a compound element of the
name Lake Istapoga. Read recognizes "Istapoga" as Maskókî, but
translates it inaccurately, as "*istî*" or "person," plus "*ak*" for "down
in the water," and "*poki*" for "finished, destroyed, killed," therefore, "a lake where a person was killed in the water." Rather the
current speakers know this lake as the place with an island in the
middle, and that the people who lived on the island mysteriously
disappeared: *istî,* 'person' or 'people' (situationally), and *pokokî(t)*
for "they are gone (dead)" or 'lost (gone away)'. They have this
memory from their grandmothers. This is the same compound word
with which the nineteenth-century half-blood George Stiggins referred to the Maskókî people, who "disappeared" as a result of the
colonialization process (George Stiggins, *Creek Indian History,*
[University of Alabama Press, 2003]).

Confusions aside, Professor Read's Florida work adds yet another important dimension to our understanding of the past. Although many etymological aspects remain unclear or controversial, this situation lends excitement to the discussion and keeps
the subject vibrant—as vibrant as the people themselves. As a social and academic product of his time, Read grasped imperfectly
the world that was symbolized in the languages he examined. He
found their taxonomic process to exhibit "little or no display of
emotion," producing "scarcely a single [name] that would appeal
to a white man's sense of beauty" (p. 78). And, yet, he reasoned
that there might be a degree of "subtlety" in the Indians' imagination. In this, he was profoundly underestimating their world and
the passion of their connection to it—a passion that is embedded
in the cultural and historical legacy that Florida carries yet today
in its fascinating Indian place names.

I. INTRODUCTION

Most of the Indian geographic names in Florida are derived from three languages of the Muskhogean family—the Seminole, the Hitchiti, and the Choctaw. The Seminole is so closely related to the Creek or Muskogee language that the two may be regarded as identical; the Hitchiti forms a linguistic union with the Mikasuki; and the Choctaw differs but slightly from the Chickasaw. If the Seminole, or the Seminole-Creek, has preserved the largest group of names, the other two languages have each transmitted a few names of more than passing interest to the linguist as well as to the historian.

Besides the names of Muskhogean origin there are two in Walton County—*Euchee Creek* and *Eucheeanna*—which recall the name of the Yuchi, a tribe affiliated with the Lower Creeks by the middle of the eighteenth century; and, what is of greater historical importance, there are a few other names that were first made known through the works of the early French or Spanish explorers, writers, and missionaries. One or two of these names are couched in the language of the Timucua, a Confederacy that once occupied the northern and central parts of Florida, whereas a few others perpetuate the memory of the Calusa Indians, who inhabited the region near Charlotte Harbor and the Caloosahatchee River.

The Seminole or Creek, the Hitchiti, the Choctaw, the Yuchi, the Timucua, and the Calusa are not the only Indian dialects that are represented in the geographic nomenclature of Florida. Many Indian names, drawn from other dialects, have been brought into the State by white men and conferred on post offices, railway stations, and settlements.

Obscure and Artificial Names. In a few cases it may be difficult to say whether a word has been derived from an Indian dialect or from some other source. Examples of this type are presented by such words as *Alafia* and *Escambia, infra*. Moreover, the origin of some names has been rendered perplexing by the deplorable American tendency to coin new names and distort old ones. *Wimauma*, for example, the name of a town in Hillsborough County, looks as if it began with Creek *wi*, "water," whereas it was actually formed, in 1903, from parts of the names (Miss) *Wi*llie, *Mau*d, and *Ma*ry, I have learned from Mr. A. A. Wadsworth, postmaster at Wimauma.

As *Wimauma* is a good illustration of an artificial name, so *Wabasso*, in Indian River County, seems to be equally typical of the obscurity caused by the reversal of the spelling of another word; for *Wabasso* is presumably formed from *Ossabaw*, the name of a sound and an island off the coast of Georgia.

Again, *Sumica*, the name of a village in Polk County, suggests with its last two syllables the possibility of a connection with Seminole-Creek *miko*, "chief." *Sumica*, however, is not of Indian origin: it is said to have been taken from the first letters of the important words in *Société Universelle: Mining (sic) Industrie, Commerce et Agriculture*—the title of a French company that owned land at the site of the present village. As to *Hypoluxo*, in Palm Beach County, so meagre is my information that I have no idea how this novel place-name arose or where it came from. Another unusual geographic name is *Yules*, in Nassau County, which, though suggestive of Creek *yàlahà*, "orange," or *yulohi*, "loose," was really given in honor of Senator D. L. Yulee, of Florida, a prominent sugar planter during the period just before and after the War between the States.[1] The present Lake Yale, in the northern part of Lake County, was formerly (1856) called *Lake Yulee*.

I have made an effort to translate those Indian geographic names, now obsolete, which are found on the Taylor War Map of 1839, and also to interpret the names of various Indians who took part in the Seminole War of 1835-1842.

---

[1] See Charles L. Norton, *A Handbook of Florida*,³ pp. 233, 367.

Pronunciation. I should have liked to include the pronunciation of the Indian geographic names; but I doubt whether I could have acquired accurate data on this phase of my subject without incurring the expense of a trip through Florida.

During the preparation of this study I have written to postmasters and other persons in Florida for information, generally historical and geographical, which might throw light on the origin and meaning of certain difficult names. It would, of course, have been unreasonable for me to expect my informants to be familiar with the Indian forms from which this or that name has sprung; but now and then I received a hint which went far towards revealing the source of a puzzling name. Take *Chuluota* and *Pithlachascotee* as illustrations of what I mean. According to local tradition, Chuluota was founded by exceptionally shrewd business men—"foxy" people, in other words—I am informed by Mrs. E. E. Tribble, of Chuluota; hence the probability is that the first element of the name is *chula*, "fox," rather than *chuli*, "pine tree." *Pithlachascotee*, too, was readily analyzed as the place where "canoes were made," after Mr. Gerben de Vries had written me that in his opinion the name had something to do with "canoes." Unfortunately, however, local tradition is often so misleading that the answers of some of my correspondents could not be verified in Seminole or in any other dialect with which I am familiar. It avails little, indeed, to be told that *Waukenah* is thought to mean "stop and rest awhile," that *Astatula* is the Seminole for "lake of sunbeams," or "lake of the sparkling moonbeams," and that *Istokpoga* is the Indian equivalent of "stinking water." Nevertheless, I am grateful for the aid that I have received, and I wish to express my thanks to the following persons:

DE VRIES, MR. GERBEN........New Port Richey
GLENN, MR. L. L..............Dania
HARTLINE, MISS MAUD........South Bay
SAMSON, MRS. P. B...........Opa Locka
SMALLWOOD, MR. C. S.........Chokoloskee
TRIBBLE, MRS. E. E...........Chuluota

The preceding list comprises the names of those citizens of Florida to whom I am most indebted. My thanks are also due to my colleague, Miss Myrtle Mestayer, for notes on the geography of certain places in Florida; to another colleague of mine, Mr. A. J. Bryan, for information that he sent me from the Harvard Library; and to Mr. Lawrence Martin, Chief of the Division of Maps, Library of Congress, as well as to Mr. John J. Cameron, Secretary of the United States Geographic Board, for the spellings of a few names on maps not within my reach; and finally, to Mrs. L. E. Pirkle, Secretary of the Department of English, Louisiana State University, for help accorded me in the reading of the proofs of my manuscript.

WILLIAM A. READ

LOUISIANA STATE UNIVERSITY
NOVEMBER 1, 1933

II. SYMBOLS AND ABBREVIATIONS

In the transcription of the Indian sources of place-names *ch* sounds as in "chin," *j* as in "gin," and a Roman *l* as in Welsh "Lloyd." *H*, when followed by a consonant, as in Creek *holahta*, is like German *ch*. Other consonants resemble the corresponding ones in English. The vowels have their continental values, except that short *i* is approximately like the vowel in "pin," and that Choctaw *u* resembles the vowel in "foot." Ă indicates a vowel like that in "nut;" *ai*, a diphthong like that in "pine." Creek *oi* or *ui*, as in *oiwa* or *uiwa*, "water," is represented by *wi*.

Most of the abbreviations will be readily understood. It should be noted, however, that *BAE* stands for *Bureau of American Ethnology*, and that *Sem.-Cr.* denotes *Seminole-Creek*.

Florida Place Names
of Indian Origin and
Seminole Personal Names

III. LIST OF GEOGRAPHIC NAMES

1. NAMES FROM THE FLORIDA DIALECTS

ALACHUA. 1. A county formed in 1824. 2. A town with a population of 865, situated on the Atlantic Coast Line and the Seaboard Air Line, in Alachua County.

Alachua was a former Seminole town, which was settled by Creeks from Oconee, Georgia, sometime in the first half of the eighteenth century. The name was afterwards applied to other settlements in the neighborhood, in which the most important town was called *Cuscowilla* or *Alachua*. (Bartram, 1778).[2]

The name *Alachua* is thought to be a derivative of Sem.-Cr. *luchuwà*, "jug," a term originally applied by the Indians to a large chasm near the present site of Gainesville, the county seat. A Creek settlement called *Allachua* is shown on a map drawn about 1715, whereas the modern spelling of the name appears on the Popple map of 1733.

ALAPATTAH. A community centre in the city of Miami, extending from N. W. Sixteenth Street to N. W. Fifty-fourth Street. The name has been used for at least ten years.

The source of *Alapattah* is Sem.-Cr. *hàlpàtà*, "alligator."

ALAQUA. A creek which rises in Walton County, and falls into Choctawhatchee Bay, in Northwest Florida.

1856. ALAQUA. Davis Map.

Alaqua is corrupted from Sem.-Cr. *hilukwà*, "sweet gum." Compare *hilukwàpi*, "sweet gum tree."

ANNUTTI ALAGGA HAMMOCK. A hammock in Hernando County.

1839. ANUTTELIGA HAMMOCK. Taylor War Map.

The name is derived from Sem.-Cr. *anàti*, "brushy place," "thicket," and *laki* or *lagi*, a variant of *laiki*, "site." A similar ending appears in the name *Topke-laké*, "fort place," an ancient Seminole town probably near Hillsborough Inlet, Florida.[3]

---

[2] Cf. F. W. Hodge, *A Handbook of American Indians North of Mexico*, 1: 34; John R. Swanton, *BAE*, Bul. 73: 180, 390.

[3] Swanton, *BAE*, Bul. 73: 405.

APALACHICOLA. 1. A town of 3,150 inhabitants on the
Apalachicola Northern Railway, in Franklin County.
2. A designation of the Chattahoochee River after its
confluence with the Flint, in Northwest Florida. 3. A
bay off the coast of Franklin County.

The name *Apalachicola* was first applied by the
Spaniards to the Lower Creeks, who formerly resided
on the Chattahoochee and Flint rivers; subsequently,
it was used as a designation of a particular town,
doubtless situated among the Lower Creeks, and now
called in Creek *tàlwa làko*, "big town."[4]

Apalachicola is composed, probably, of Hitchiti *apa-
lahchi*, "on the other side," and *okli*, "people"; hence
"those people residing on the other side, shore, or river."

APOPKA. 1. A lake in Orange County; a part of this
body of water extends over into Lake County.

1839. LAKE AHAPOPKA. Taylor War Map.

2. A town of 1,134 inhabitants on the Seaboard
Air Line, in Orange County. Apopka is noted in Sidney
Lanier's *Florida* (1876), pp. 312-313, as a small settle-
ment near Lake Apopka.

The source of this name is Cr. *aha*, "potato," and
papka, "eating place," from *papità*, "to eat"—"potato
eating place."

APOXSEE. A station on the Florida East Coast Railroad,
in Osceola County.

1930. APOXSEE. Sectional Map of Florida.

Sem.-Cr. *àpaksi*, "to-morrow," is the source of this
name.

ARIPEKA. A hamlet of thirty-three inhabitants in Passo
county; a recent name.

Sam Jones, a famous Mikasuki chief, went by the
name of *Aripeka* or *Arpeika*. There are other insignifi-
cant variants of his name, such as *Apiaka, Apeiaka,* and
Appiaca.

In 1841, the year before the close of the Seminole
War, Aripeka occupied the region near the mouth of the
Kissimee River and the eastern border of Lake Okecho-
bee. He is said to have had seventeen warriors and a
large number of women and children in his band. He
was then about seventy-eight years old.

---

[4] Swanton, *BAE*, Bul. 73: 109, 129-130.

Associated with Sam Jones there was a Creek chief who was known as *The Prophet,* though one of his Indian names, *Otulke-Thloko,* is a corruption of *hotàlgi làko,* and signifies "Big Wind Clan" (chief).

Another name that the Prophet bore was *Hilis Hadjo,* "Crazy Medicine," from Cr. *hilis,* "medicine," and *hajo,* "crazy."

The name *Aripeka* is possibly corrupted from Cr. *abihka,* "pile at the base," "heap at the root," an ancient Creek town near the upper Coosa River. The name was conferred on the town because "in the contest for supremacy its warriors heaped up a pile of scalps, covering the base of the war-pole."[5]

The United States Post-Office Guide for 1904, p. 366, spells the name of this town *Arbeka.*

According to another view, the Abihka were an ancient Muskhogean tribe residing in the Talladega Valley of Alabama, who received their name because of the singular manner in which they expressed assent or approbation. Still another etymology would connect *Abihka* with Choctaw *aiabika,* "unhealthful place."[6]

ATTAPULGAS. 1. A creek in Gadsden County. 2. A former Seminole town on the Ochlockonee River bore this name.

> ATTAPULGA. Norton, *op. cit.,* Map, p. 31.

> Attapulgas is derived from Cr. *atàpha,* "dogwood," and *-àlgi,* "grove."

BITHLO. A village of 128 inhabitants on the Florida East Coast Railroad, in Orange County.

> 1930. BITHLO. Sectional Map.

> The origin of the name is Sem.-Cr. *pilo,* "canoe." The discrepancy between *pilo* and *Bithlo* is largely due to the fact that the Sem.-Cr. voiceless "l" was often written *thl.*

CHARLEY APOPKA CREEK. An affluent of Peace Creek, in Hardee County.

> 1856. BIG CHARLEY POPKA CREEK. Davis Map.

> *Charley* is corrupted from Sem. *chalo,* "trout," and *Apapka* from Sem. *papka,* "eating place"—"the place where trout are eaten." Cf. *Little Charley Apopka Creek* and *Tsala Apopka Lake, infra.*

---

[5] A. S. Gatschet, *A Migration Legend of the Creek Indians,* 1: 124-125.
[6] Swanton, *BAE,* Bul. 73: 251-252.

Sprague, in his *Florida War*, p. 282, mentions the beauty of the Charlo-Popka country, a name which he renders by "trout-eating ponds."

CHASSAHOWITZKA. 1. A short, broad stream in the extreme southwestern corner of Citrus County. 2. A point off the coast of Citrus County. 3. A swamp in Hernando County.

> 1839. CHASAHOWITSKA R. Taylor Map.
>
> 1856. CHASEHOWITSKA R. Davis Map.

The name signifies "hanging pumpkins," from Sem. *chasi*, "pumpkins," and *wiski*, "hanging loose."

The fruit of pumpkin vines, which climb among the branches of the trees, is highly esteemed by the Seminoles. During the Seminole War the American troops amused themselves by firing at the stems and bringing the pumpkins to the ground.[7]

CHATTAHOOCHEE. A station on the Seaboard Air Line, in Gadsden County.

> 1870. CHATTAHOOCHEE. Colton Map.

The name was taken from that of the well-known river in Georgia, in the bed of which pictured rocks are found. On the Early Map of Georgia, dated 1818, the name *Chattohochee* is rendered by "flowered stone."[8]

The exact source is Sem.-Cr. *chàto*, "rock," and *huchi*, "marked."

CHILLOCAHATCHEE. A stream flowing southward through Hardee and De Soto Counties.

The name signifies "horse creek," being derived from Sem.-Cr. *chulako*, "horse," and *hàchi*, "creek." *Chulako* itself is composed of Sem.-Cr. *ichu*, "deer," and *làko*, "large."

CHIPCO. 1. A lake in Putnam County, near Interlachen. 2. A station on the Orange Belt Railroad, in Pasco County.

> 1892. CHIPCO. Norton, *op. cit.*, p. 283.

Chipko was the name of a Seminole settlement at Catfish Lake, near Lake Okeechobee. The settlement bore the name of Chief Chipko, who was with Osceola at the Dade Massacre in 1835.

Chipko is a corruption of Seminole *chàpko*, "tall."

---

[7] Cf. Minnie Moore-Wilson, *The Seminoles of Florida*, p. 82.

[8] See Swanton, *BAE*, Bul. 73: Plate 9.

CHITE-HATCHEE. A stream shown on Sprague's sketch (1841) and situated in what is now Monroe County. The name is intended for Sem.-Cr. *chito*, "snake," and *hàchi*, "river"—"snake river."

CHOCONIKLA. Just north of the present site of Wauchula, in what is now Hardee County, there was a fort called *Chokonikla*. The name is taken from Sem.-Cr. *chuko*, "house," and *nikli*, "burnt"—"burnt house."

　1856. CHOKONIKLA. Jeff Davis Map.

Choconikla was also the name of a Seminole town, on the west side of the Apalachicola River, in Decatur County, Georgia. This town had about sixty warriors in 1820.

CHOCTAWHATCHEE. A name found several times in the geographical nomenclature of Florida, as follows: 1. The *Choctawhatchee River* forming the boundary between Washington and Walton Counties. 2. The *Choctawhatchee National Forest* extending across Okaloosa County into Santa Rosa on the west and Walton County on the east. 3. *Choctawhatchee Bay* lying in the southern part of Okaloosa and Walton Counties.

　The first element in *Choctawhatchee* has arisen through confusion of the tribal name *Choctaw* with *Chatot*, the name of a Muskhogean tribe which settled in the neighborhood of Mobile, Alabama, about 1706. The meaning of *Chatot* is unknown, and *Choctaw* is equally obscure. The second element of *Choctawhatchee* is derived from Creek *hàchi*, "river."

CHOKOLOSKEE. A town of 131 inhabitants near the southern boundary of Collier County.

　The name is corrupted from Sem.-Cr. *chuko*, "house," and *liski*, "old"—therefore, "old house."

　1856. CHOKOLISKA. Jeff Davis Map.

CHUCCOCHARTS HAMMOCKS. The name of an area approximately thirteen miles long and eight broad, in the southeastern corner of Hernando County.

　1930. CHUCCOCHARTS HAMMOCKS. Sectional Map.

　The source of this name is Sem.-Cr. *chuko*, "house," and *chati*, "red"—"red house." Sprague, in his *Florida War*, p. 278, spells it *Chocochate*.

Bernard Romans, in *A Concise Natural History of Florida*, 1775, p. 281, mentions a Creek town by the name of *New Eufaula*, which Swanton, *BAE*, Bul. 73: 403, believes to be identical with the one subsequently called *Red House* or *Red Town*. The name of the hammock was taken from that of the town, in which the houses were daubed with red clay.

CHULUOTA. A town with a population of 243 on the Florida East Coast Line, in Seminole County.

1892. CHULUOTA. Norton Map, p. 68.

Chuluota is probably composed of Sem. *chula*, "fox," and *huti*, "den." If, however, the name happens to be of Choctaw origin, it is composed of *chula*, "foxes," and *àtta*, "to live,"—that is, "a place where foxes are common."

The translation "beautiful view," as recorded by Gannett, is apparently due to an erroneous association of the first element of the name with Mexican Spanish *chulo(a)*, "pretty," "graceful," etc.[9]

CRYSTAL RIVER. A town with a population of 869 on the Atlantic Coast Line, in Citrus County; shown on the Colton Map, 1870.

The town takes its name from that of a stream recorded on the Taylor War Map, 1839, as *Weewa-hi-i-aca* or *Crystal River*. On the Davis Map, 1856, the Indian name has disappeared and *Crystal R.* alone is found. The *Sectional Map* of 1930 records the stream as *Crystal River*. Norton, p. 376, gives the Indian name in the form *Wewakiahakee* and translates it by "clear water."

The spelling of the name on the Taylor War Map furnishes the clue to the correct translation of the name: *Weewa-hi-i-aca* is derived from Sem.-Cr. *wiwa*, "water," and *haiyayàki*, "clear," "shining"—freely, then, "crystal water."

EAST MYAKKA. A station on the Seaboard Air Line, in Manatee County, just south of Myakka City; recorded by Rand McNally, 1931. Cf. *Port Mayaca, infra.*

---

[9] Henry Gannett, "The Origin of Certain Place Names in the United States," *U. S. Geological Survey*,[2] Bul. 258: 81.

ECHASHOTEE. A river that empties into the Gulf, just south of the Pithlochascotee, in Pasco County.

    1839. ANCLOTE or ETHAS-HOTEE R. Taylor Map.

    1856. ECHASHOTEE R. Davis Map.

    1870. ECHASHOTEE R. Colton Map.

On the Taylor Map this stream is confused with the Anclote, which lies farther south in Pasco county.

    Echashotee is derived from Sem.-Cr. *ichaswà*, "beaver," and *huti*, "house."

ECONFINE. 1. A river passing through the southeastern corner of Washington County, running through Bay County, and falling into North Bay, on the coast of Bay County. 2. A river flowing southward through Taylor County and emptying into the Gulf. 3. A station, Econfena, on the Live Oak, Perry and Gulf Railway, in Taylor County. 4. A village, Econfina, with 137 inhabitants, in Bay County, *mail* Bennett; referred to in Lanier's *Florida* (1876), p. 318, as a small settlement on Econfina River.

    1839. ECONFINEE RIVER. (Taylor Co.) Taylor Map.

    1856. ECONFENEE R. (Taylor Co.) Davis Map.

    1856. ESCONFENEE C. (Wash. Co.) Davis Map.

    1870. ECONFINA CR. (Wash. Co.) Colton Map.

    1870. ECONFENEE R. (Taylor Co.) Colton Map.

    1930. ECONFENA R. (Taylor Co.) Sectional Map.

The first element of this name is perfectly clear: it is the familiar Creek *ikàna*, "earth." If the second element could safely be considered an abbreviation of Cr. *finoki*, "shaking," then the translation would be "swampy grounds"; but unfortunately for such an assumption, the early spellings of the river name all point unmistakably to Creek *fina*, "a footlog," "a bridge," as the source of the second element. The name signifies, then, "natural (earth) bridge"; an apt name because about fifteen miles up from the mouth of the Econfina, in Taylor County, there is a natural bridge which obstructs navigation.[10]

I note that the term *fina* appears in *Chulafinnee*, the name of a hamlet in Cleburne County, Alabama, which Gannett, *Geol. Bulletin* 258: 81, renders incorrectly by

---

[10] Cf. Norton, *op. cit.*, p. 93.

"Red Fox." In this name the first element is Creek *chuli,* "pine tree," and the second is, as has been observed, *fina,* "footlog"—hence "pine log crossing." In the Creek dialect "red fox" would be *chula chati.*

ECONLOCKHATCHEE. A river rising in the southeastern part of Orange County, and flowing north and east into the St. Johns River, in Seminole County.

The diversity of forms is so remarkable that an accurate translation of this name is very difficult. Here are some of the variant spellings:

1839. ECON-LIKE HATCHEE. Taylor Map.

1856. ECONTIKAHOCHEE. Surveyor General's Map of Florida.

1859. ECONTIKAHOOCHEE. U. S. Gov. Map of Florida.

1886. ECONTOCHATCHIE. G. L. O. Map of Florida.

1923. ECONTOCKHATCHEE. Map of Florida, Dept. of Agriculture.

1927. ECONLOCKHATCHEE. U. S. Geog. Board.

1913. CONTOOHATCHEE. Geol. Survey, Water Supply Paper, Wash.

1931. CONTOOHATCHEE. Rand McNally Map of Florida.

However obscure this name may be, it shows certain features that are easily interpreted. The first element in all the forms except those beginning with *Contoo* can hardly be anything but Cr. *ikàna,* "earth," "ground"; and the last element in all the forms must be Cr. *hàchi,* "river." Again, the form *Contoohatchee* appears too late to deserve serious consideration: *Contoo* probably being due to confusion of *Econtoc*—or *Econtock*—with *kunti,* "coontie," the name the Seminoles apply to the flour they make from the root of a cycadaceous plant *(Bamia integrifolia).*

It is my belief that the original meaning of the name is concealed in *Econ-like Hatchee,* the form recorded on the Taylor War Map of 1839, which I take to be the equivalent of "earth-mound river." Cr. *laiki* signifies "site," but may be rendered more freely by "mound." Hawkins (1799), in the *Georgia Historical Society Collections,* III, 39, renders *E-cun-ligee* by "mounds of earth."

EFAW. A station on the Florida East Coast Railroad, in Okeechobee County.

> 1899. EFAW. Century Atlas.

Cr. *ifa,* "dog," is the source.

EMATHLA. A station on the Jacksonville, Gainesville and Gulf Railroad, in Marion County. This name was probably given in honor of Charley Emathla, a Seminole chief who was murdered in 1835 by Osceola's warriors because he had consented to emigrate from Florida.

> 1839. CHARLEY EMATHLA'S TOWN. Taylor War Map.
> 1930. EMATHLA. Sectional Map, Dept. of Agri.

Emathla is the Sem.-Cr. *imala,* a busk-title which may be rendered by "leader," "councilor," "assistant."

ESTIFFANULGA. A hamlet of ninety-seven inhabitants situated on the east bank of the Apalachicola River in Liberty County: a name apparently of recent application.

The source is probably Cr. *Isfanàlgi,* a corruption of Cr. *Ispani,* "Spaniard," and *-àlgi,* "clan," the designation of one of the nine clans of the Creek Confederacy.

EUCHEE. The name of a creek, a tributary of the Choctawhatchee River, in Walton County. The stream is traced on the Davis Map, 1856, though the name is not recorded.

Euchee is intended for *Yuchi;* cf. *Eucheeanna, infra.*

EUCHEEANNA. A Scotch settlement in Walton County.

> 1856. UCHEE ANNA. Davis Map.
> 1870. UCHEE ANNA. Colton Map.
> 1892. EUCHEE ANNA. Norton Map, p. 100.

The word is derived from the name *Yuchi* with the aid of the suffix *-ana,* an adaptation of the Latin feminine ending *-ana.*

Yuchi is the name of an Indian tribe incorporated with the Creek confederacy, its signification probably being "at a distance," from Yuchi *yu,* "at a distance," and *chi,* "sitting down."

FAHKAHHATCHEE. A river in Collier County, falling into Fakkahhatchee Bay, near Fakkahhatchee Island.

On Sprague's *Sketch* (1841-1842) the name is spelled *Faka-hatchee*. *Fahkahhatchee* signifies "vine river," or perhaps "clay river," the Seminole source being either *(i)fàkà,* "vine," or *faki,* "clay," and *hàchi,* "river."

A little farther south another stream by the name of *Fahkahhatchoochee* falls into the waters surrounding Ten Thousand Islands. This name, which is recorded on the Davis Map, 1856, and the Colton Map, 1870, signifies "Little Fahkahhatchee."

FENHOLLOWAY. 1. A river flowing southwest through Taylor County into the Gulf. 2. A hamlet with a population of thirty-four situated on the Live Oak, Perry and Gulf Railroad, in Taylor County; recorded on the map in N. O. Winter's *Florida: The Land of Enchantment* (1918).

> 1839. FENAHALLOWI (RIVER). Taylor War Map.
>
> 1856. FENHALLOWĀY R. Davis Map.
>
> 1870. FINHOLLOWAY R. Colton Map.
>
> 1892. FENHOLLOWAY R. Norton Map, p. 93.

Finhalui was a former Creek settlement (1832), probably in Wayne County, Georgia.

The source of *Fenholloway (Finhalui)* is Sem.-Cr. *fina,* "footlog," and *hàlwi,* "high"—"high footlog."

FISH-EATING CREEK. A stream rising in Highlands County, flowing southward, and crossing the northern boundary of Glades County, whence it turns eastward to empty into Lake Okeechobee, near Lakeport.

> 1839. THLOTHLOPOPKA-HATCHEE or FISH EATING CREEK. Taylor Map.
>
> 1870. TLATHLOPOPKAHATCHEE R. Colton Map.
>
> 1892. FISH EATING CR. Norton Map, p. 23.
>
> 1930. FISH EATING CREEK. Sectional Map.

The Seminole term for this stream is *làlo,* "fish," *papka,* "eating place," and *hàchi,* "creek," or "river"— "the stream where fish are eaten." In the spellings of 1839 and 1870 the *thl* indicates voiceless *l.*

HALPATIOKEE. A river in Martin County.

    1839. ALPATIOHEE CR. Taylor Map.

    1839. CF. AL-PA-TI-OKEE SWAMP. Taylor Map.

    1856. N. HALPAHTIOKEE R. Davis Map.

    1856. S. HALPAHTIOKEE R. Davis Map.

The spelling on the Taylor Map with -*h*- is manifestly erroneous.

The meaning of the name is "alligator stream," and the source is Hitchiti *hàlpàtà,* "alligator," and *oki,* "water."

HATCHINEHA. A lake in the northeastern corner of Polk County. Sem.-Cr. *àchinàho,* "cypress tree," is the source of the name.

On the Taylor Map, 1839, the Davis Map, 1856, and the Colton Map, 1870, this body of water is designated as *Cypress L.* On the Map that accompanies Norton's *Florida*[3] (1892), the name of the lake is recorded as *Hatchenana;* on the Sectional Map, Department of Agriculture, 1930, the modern spelling is used.

HIALEAH. A town of 2,600 inhabitants, situated on the Seaboard Air Line, in Dade County.

The name *Hialeah* is said to signify "beautiful prairie," and to have been selected by an Indian chief, named *Willie Willie,* whose village occupied the site of the town until about 1929. This explanation is probably correct, though it indicates a serious corruption of Sem.-Cr. *haiyakpo,* "prairie," and *hili,* "pretty."

HICPOCHEE. A lake on the southeastern boundary of Glades County—"called by the Indians Haik-pachee."— Sprague, *Florida War* (Nov. 25, 1841), p. 334.

    1856. HICKPOCHEE L. Davis Map.

The name is contracted from Sem.-Cr. *haiyakpo,* "prairie," and -*chi,* "little"—"little prairie lake."

HILLSBORO RIVER OR LOCKTSAPOPKA. A river flowing southward and falling into Hillsboro Bay, which forms the northern end of Tampa Bay, in Hillsboro County.

    1856. HILLSBORO R. or LOCKTSAPOPKA R. Davis Map.

    1870. HILLSBORO or LOCKTSAPOPKA R. Colton Map.

If the spelling on the Davis and Colton maps is trustworthy, the Indian name of this stream is derived from Cr. *lokcha*, "acorns," and *papka*, "eating place"—"the place where acorns are eaten."

HILOLO. A town of 500 inhabitants, on the Florida East Coast Railroad, in Okeechobee County; a comparatively modern place-name.

The source of *Hilolo* is Sem.-Cr. *àlolo*, "long-billed curlew" (*Numenius Americanus* Wils.).

HOLOPAW. A town with a population of 1,702, on the Florida East Coast Railroad, in Osceola County: recorded on the map in Nevin O. Winter's *Florida*. Minnie Moore-Wilson, in *The Seminoles of Florida*, p. 111, translates *holopaw* by "walk (pavement)." The word is evidently connected with Sem.-Cr. *hàlatipuichita*, "to haul or draw" as with a horse, a term composed of *hàlatità*, "to draw," and *puichità*, "to cause." *Holopaw* signifies, then, the place where something is hauled.

HOMOSASSA. 1. A short, clear river in Citrus County.

1839. HOMOSASSA R. Taylor Map.

1856. HOMOSASSA R. Davis Map.

2. A village with 487 inhabitants, on the Atlantic Coast Line, and on the Homosassa River.

1856. HOMOSASSA. Davis Map.

3. Homosassa Springs. A village with 300 inhabitants, on the Atlantic Coast Line, near Homosassa. 4. Homosassa Bay, Homosassa Islands, and Homosassa Point, all off the coast of Citrus County.

In 1836 there was a Seminole settlement called *Homosassa* at or near the site of the present town of this name.

Homosassa is composed of Sem.-Cr. *homo*, "pepper," and *sasi*, "is there"—that is to say, "a place where wild pepper grows."

IAMONIA. 1. A lake in the northern part of Leon County. 2. A village of 187 inhabitants, situated near the lake; a small settlement, according to Sidney Lanier's *Florida*, p. 371.

Hiamonee was the name of an ancient Seminole town, situated on the east bank of the Ochlockonee River, five miles from the Georgia line. This name seems to be connected with the tribal name *Yamassee,* which signifies "mild, peaceable," from Creek *yàmàsi.* Swanton cites the form *Yamane* from a map of 1744 as the name of a Yamassee settlement near Mobile. The resemblance between *Iamonia* and *Yamane* is perhaps convincing evidence of their kinship. The Yamassee, after their defeat by the whites in 1716, were finally absorbed by the Creeks and the Seminoles.

ILLAHAW. A station on the Florida East Coast Railroad, in Osceola County. The name is taken from Seminole *yàlahà,* "orange."

IOLA. 1. A village with a population of 212, in Gulf County, recorded on the Davis Map of 1856.

An ancient Seminole town formerly occupied the site of the present Iola, near the junction of the Chipola River with the Apalachicola. This Seminole town was called *Iolee, Yauollee,* and less accurately, *Yanollee.* The spelling *Yauollee* seems to point to Creek *Yahola* as the source of the name. *Yahola* was the cry uttered by the attendants while the chiefs were taking the black drink. Originally, however, *Yahola* was the name of a male deity to whom appeals were made in case of sickness, or any serious emergency. The name *Yahola* formed a part of many Creek war titles, as in *Yahola fiksiko,* "heartless Yahola," *Yahola hajo,* "crazy or mad Yahola," and *àsi yahola,* "black drink Yahola." Cf. the meaning of the name *Osceola, infra.*[11]

ISTACHATTA. A town with a population of 227, in Hernando County; recorded on the map in Norton's *Florida*[3] (1892), p. 34.

The word is composed of Sem. *isti,* "man," and *chati,* "red"—"Indian," or "red man."

ISTOKPOGA. 1. A lake in Highlands County; recorded on the Taylor War Map, 1839. 2. Lake Istokpoga, a station on the Seaboard Air Line, just north of the lake; recorded on the Sectional Map, 1930. 3. A hamlet of ninety-nine inhabitants on the Atlantic Coast Line, west of the lake; recorded by Rand McNally, 1931.

---

[11] On *Yahola,* see Gatschet, *op. cit.,* 1: 163; 2: 57, 58; and Swanton, *BAE,* **Rep.** 42: 101, 485.

Istokpoga was an upper Creek settlement, probably near the present Eastaboga, in Talladega County, Alabama. The latter name signifies "where people reside," the elements being Cr. *isti,* "people," and *poga,* from *apokita,* "to reside."

The *k* is said to be silent in the local pronunciation of *Istokpoga:* but whether the two names are identical in meaning is, in view of the persistence of the *k*-forms of *istokpoga,* more than doubtful. I suggest that this name is derived from Sem. *isti,* "person," *ak,* "down in the water," and *poki,* "finished," "destroyed," "killed," from *poyita,* "to finish," etc. Cf. the place-name *Loachapoka,* in Lee County, Alabama, from *locha* "turtle," and *poka,* "killing place." *Istokpoga* signifies, then, the lake where a person was killed in the water.

ISTOPOGAYOXEE, or REEDY LAKE. A Lake in Polk County.

> 1892. ETSOPOGAYOXEE. Norton's Map.
>
> 1930. ISTOPOGAYOXEE. Sectional Map.

This name is derived from Sem.-Cr. *isti,* "people," *poga,* "reside," from Cr. *apokita,* and *i-uksa,* "at the end of it" *(i-).*

ITABO. A station on the Atlantic Coast Line, near Citronella, in Citrus County. The Rand McNally map of 1930 records the name.

Ranjel, in his narrative of De Soto's expedition, mentions *Itaba* in the following language:

> "On Friday, August 20, 1540, the Governor De-Soto and his people left Coça, and there stayed behind a Christian named Feryada, a Levantine: and they slept the next night beyond Talimachusy, and the next day in a heavy rain they went to Itaba, a large village along a fine river, and there they bought some Indian women, which were given them in exchange for looking-glasses and knives.
>
> "Monday, August 30, 1540, the Governor left Itaba, and came by nightfall to an oak wood; and the next day they were at Ulibahali, a very fine village close to a large river."[12]

The Gentleman of Elvas, in his account of De Soto's expedition, uses the spelling *Ytaua* instead of *Itaba.*[13]

---

[12] Ranjel, in *Narratives of De Soto,* 2: 113.
[13] *Narratives of De Soto,* 1: 84.

Ytaua is probably a corruption of Cr. *itàlwa*, "town," "tribe." The other places that the expedition passed through may likewise be interpreted in Creek with the exception of Coça, which is probably the Choctaw *kūshak*, "cane." Thus *Talimachusy*, "new town," is Cr. *tàlwa*, "town," and *muchàsi*, "new"; *Ulibahali* is intended for Cr. *Holiwahali*, a compound of *holi*, "war," and *àwahali*, "to divide out," *holiwahali* being the name of a former Upper Creek town situated on the Tallapoosa River. According to another interpretation, *Ulibahali* is the Alabama *oli*, "town," and Hitchiti *bahali*, "down stream."

At any rate, the present *Itabo*, in Citrus County, may be due to a reminiscence of the ancient *Itaba*.

ITCHEPUCKESASSA. A river in the northeastern part of Hillsborough County.

> 1839. HICHIPUCKSASSA (settlement). Taylor Map.

> 1870. ICHEPUCKSASSA (settlement). Colton Map.

The source of this name is *hichi*, "tobacco," *pàkpàki*, "blossoms," and *sasi*, "to be there"—"where there are (wild) tobacco blossoms," or, more freely, as in Norton's translation, *Handbook*[3] (1892), p. 375, "tobacco field."

ITCHETUCKNEE. Two large springs uniting in a river which forms a part of the southwestern boundary of Columbia County. This short stream is about twenty miles southwest of Lake City, and empties into the Santa Fe River.

Taylor's War Map of 1839 records the name of a spring as *Itchetucknee*. Since Sprague, *Florida War*, p. 272, gives *Hitchatuckenne Springs* (1841), I am inclined to accept this as a form quite close to the original source. Perhaps the name signifies "blistered tobacco," from Sem.-Cr. *hichi*, "tobacco," and *tàkani*, "blistered."

KOLOKEE. A station on the Florida East Coast Railroad, in Seminole County; a name of comparatively recent application. The source is Sem.-Cr. *kulki*, "lamp."

KOSTA, OR TIGER LAKE. A body of water in the eastern part of Polk County: recorded on the Davis map, 1856, merely as *Tiger L.;* on Norton's Map, p. 77, with both names.

Kosta is a corruption of Sem.-Cr. *kachà*, "panther," or colloquially "tiger."

LACOOCHEE. A town of 1,427 inhabitants, on the Atlantic Coast Line, in the extreme northeastern part of Pasco County.

> 1892. LACOOCHEE. Norton, *op. cit.*, p. 75.

The town is situated on the Withlacoochee River, and took its name in all probability from that of this stream, *Lacoochee* being merely a shortened form of *Withlacoochee, infra.* The town of Withla, *infra,* on the other hand, owes its name to the omission of the last two syllables of *Withlacoochee.*

LITTLE CHARLEY APOPKA. A creek, an affluent of Peace Creek, in the northern end of Hardee County. Cf. *Charley Apopka Creek, supra.*

LOCHAPOPKA. A lake in the southern part of Polk County.

> 1856. LOCHA POPKA L. Davis Map.
> 1892. L. LOCHAPOPKA. Norton, *op. cit.*, p. 77.

This name signifies a place where turtles or terrapins are eaten. The source is Sem. *locha*, "turtle," "terrapin," and *papka*, "eating place," from *papità*, "to eat." The Seminole is fond both of terrapins and of turtles, which he usually broils in their shells.

LOCKTSAPOPKA RIVER. See *Hillsboro River, supra.*

LOCHLOOSA. 1. A lake in the southeastern corner of Alachua County.

> 1839. LAKE LULHLOSA. Taylor Map.
> 1870. L. LULHOOSA. Colton Map.
> 1892. L. LOCKLOOSA. Norton, *op. cit.*, p. 3.
> 1930. L. LOCHLOOSA. Sectional Map.

2. A village of 120 inhabitants on the Seaboard Air Line, situated on the eastern boundary of the lake.

This is a Choctaw word, its source being *luksi*, "terrapin," and *lusa*, "black"—"black terrapin." The early spellings are hopelessly corrupt.

LOKOSEE. A village of 370 inhabitants, on the Florida East Coast Railway, in Osceola County.

> 1930. LOKOSEE. Sectional Map.

Lokosee looks like a play upon the Seminole word for "bear" (ursus)—*nokosi.*

LOXAHATCHEE. 1. A river with two branches situated near Jupiter, in the northeastern corner of Palm Beach County.

> 1839. LOCHA HATCHEE. Taylor Map.
>
> 1841. LOCHA-HATCHIE. Sprague, *op. cit.*, p. 378.

2. A hamlet with 123 inhabitants, situated on West Palm Beach Canal, in Palm Beach County; recorded by Rand McNally, 1931.

This name signifies "turtle river," the source being Sem.-Cr. *locha,* "turtle," and *hàchi,* "river."

MATTLACHA PASS. A shallow strip of water east of Big Pine Island, in Charlotte Harbor, Lee County.

Mattlacha seems to be a derivative of Sem.-Cr. *imala,* "warriors' assistant," and *-uchi,* "little." Ematlochee's Town was a former Creek settlement, thirty miles east of Apalachicola.

Moreover, an Indian chief by the name of *Emathlochee* was one of those who endorsed the treaty of Fort Moultrie, on September 18, 1823, a treaty which allotted certain reservations of land to the Florida Indians: see Sprague, *op. cit.*, pp. 22, 24.

The Seminole voiceless *l* is indicated by *-ttl-* in *Mattlacha.*

The Creek war and busk title *imala* is variously rendered by "leader," "assistant," "messenger," and "disciplinarian."

MIAKKA. A village of 161 inhabitants, situated near the northeastern boundary of Sarasota County; recorded by Norton, 1892, and by *The Century Atlas*, 1899. Cf. *Myakka City, infra.*

MIAMI. 1. A city with a population of 110,637, situated at the mouth of a short river of the same name and on Biscayne Bay, in Dade County. Miami was not incorporated until 1896. Its railroads are the Florida East Coast and the Seaboard Air Line.

Some other places in Dade County have taken the name *Miami*—Miami Beach (pop. 6,494), Miami Shores (pop. 612), and Miami Springs (pop. 402).

Taylor's War Map shows the Miami River and also Fort Dallas, the latter a military post established in January, 1838, and abandoned in June, 1858. This fort occupied the present site of Miami. In 1880 there was a Seminole settlement with sixty-three inhabitants on Little Miami River, about ten miles north of the present site of Miami.[14]

Writing in 1575 Fontanedo mentions a lake by the name of *Mayaimi*, which he translates by "very large." This name, of which *Miami* is a variant, may be a compound of Choctaw *maiha*, "wide," and *mih*, "it is so."[15] By *Laguna de Mayaimi* Fontanedo meant what is now called *Lake Okeechobee*.[16] Aviles, on his expedition up the St. Johns River in 1566, called this lake *Maymi*.[17]

MICANOPY. 1. A town of 725 inhabitants, in Alachua County, situated at the junction of the Atlantic Coast Line with the Jacksonville, Gainesville and Gulf Railroad. This town is shown on the Davis Map of 1856; moreover, a military post bearing the name *Micanopy* was founded here by the United States government on April 30, 1837. 2. Micanopy Junction, a station on the Atlantic Coast Line, four miles east of Micanopy.

At the outbreak of the Seminole War in 1835 the head chief of the Seminoles was Mikonopi, who lived at Okehumpkee just west of Lake Astatula in what is now Lake County. Micanopy joined Osceola in refusing to sign the agreement of April 23, 1835, in accordance with which the Seminoles were to emigrate and relinquish their lands to the United States. On December 28, 1835, Micanopy and his band massacred a detachment of United States troops near the present site of St. Catherine in what is now Sumter County. Of the total American force, consisting of 110 men, only one or two escaped with their lives, and their leader, Major Francis L. Dade, is said to have been slain by Chief Micanopy himself. This combat marks the virtual beginning of

---

[14] MacCauley, in *BAE*, Rep. 5: 478.

[15] Cf. Woodbury Lowery, *The Spanish Settlements Within the Present Limits of the United States*, 2: 441; Swanton, *BAE*, Bul. 73: 30.

[16] Lowery, *Spanish Settlements*, 1: 62.

[17] Lowery, *ibid.*, 2: 258, 262.

the Seminole War (1835-1842), which resulted in the expenditure of approximately $10,000,000 and the loss of thousands of lives.

The name *Mikonopi* signifies "head chief," being derived from Sem. *miko*, "chief," and *onàpà*, "above," "upper."

MICCO. A village with a population of 274, on the Florida East Coast Railway, in Brevard County. Sem.-Cr. *miko* signifies "chief." The village was probably named after some Indian whose name was *Miko*.

An aged chief by the name of Micco, who had been captured in the Everglades by Major Childs, tried to find Coacoochee and induce him to surrender.[18]

MICCOSUKEE. 1. A town of 1,054 inhabitants in Leon County, on the western shore of Lake Miccosukee. 2. A lake situated in Jefferson County, about nineteen miles northeast of Tallahassee. This lake is approximately fifteen miles long and four miles across at its widest point.

The Mackay Blake Map of 1840 records the name as *L. Mikasukie.*

The Mikasuki formed an important branch of the Seminole tribe, but whether they were more closely related to the Hitchiti or to the Chiaha cannot now be determined.

The first settlement of the Mikasuki in Florida was in Jefferson County, near the lake; subsequently they moved to a site near Greenville, in Madison County. This band of Indians played a conspicuous part in the Seminole War of 1835-1842. The Mikasuki spoke a dialect closely resembling Hitchiti, and came into Florida from the Sawokli towns of the Lower Chattahoochee River, in Alabama. *Sawokli* is composed of Hitchiti *sawi*, "raccoon," and *okli*, "people."

Miccosukee is usually rendered by "chiefs of the hog clan," from Hitchiti *miki*, "chief," and *suki*, "hogs," but the name may have been corrupted from Hitchiti *mikasuki*, "hog eaters."

MYAKKA CITY. 1. A town of 457 inhabitants, on the Seaboard Air Line, in Manatee County. See the Rand McNally map of 1930. 2. A lake on the Myakka River,

---

[18] See Sprague, *op. cit.*, p. 258.

in Sarasota County. In 1856 this body of water was called *Lake Mayaco*, according to Brinton. 3. A river, rising in Manatee County, flowing through Sarasota County, and emptying into Charlotte Harbor: recorded as *Miaco R.* on the Purcell map (1792), and as *Myakka R.* on the Davis Map of 1856. The spelling of the United States Geographic Board is *Miakka*.

The name *Myakka* (Miakka) is identical with *Mayaca*, for which see *Port Mayaca, infra.*[19]

NARCOOSSEE. A village with a population of 212, on the Atlantic Coast Line, near the northern boundary of Osceola County. This name, which is recorded by Norton, *op. cit.*, p. 71, seems to be identical with that of a former Cherokee settlement situated in Habersham County, Georgia, and variously designated as *Naguchee, Nacoochee, Nacochee, Noccocsee,* and *Cauchi.* A valley in this county still bears the name *Nacoochee.* The name cannot be translated.[20]

Tradition has it that Nacoochee was an Indian princess who loved Laceola, the chief of a hostile tribe.

According to information recently furnished me by Mr. F. A. Stroup, postmaster at Narcoossee, the name *Narcoossee* is thought to signify "Little brown bear." *Narcoossee*, then, is in all probability merely a corruption of Seminole *nokosi* or *nokusi*, "bear *(ursus)*." "Little bear" is *nokosuchi* in Seminole, whereas "brown bear" is *nokosyahà*, literally "wolf bear."

NOCATEE. A town with a population of 1,312 inhabitants, on the Atlantic Coast Line, in De Soto County. This name is merely the Seminole *nakiti*, "*what is it?*"

1892. NOCATEE. Norton, *op. cit.*, page 22.

OCHEESEE. 1. A hamlet in the northeastern corner of Calhoun County.

1870. OCHESEE. Colton Map.

1892. OCHEESEE. Norton, *op. cit.*, p. 388.

1930. OCHEESEE L. Sectional Map.

2. A lake near Grand Ridge, Jackson County.

1930. OCHEESEE L. Sectional Map.

---

[19] Cf. Daniel G. Brinton, *Notes on the Floridian Peninsula, etc.*, p. 115.
[20] See James Mooney, *BAE*, Rep. 19, Part 1, pp. 197, 416.

A former Seminole town was situated at or near the present site of Ocheesee. This name is derived from Sem.-Cr. *ochi*, "hickory," and *isi*, "leaf."

Most of the inhabitants of Ocheesee are thought to have come from Hickory Ground, a former Creek settlement on the left bank of the Coosa, two miles above the fork of the river, in Alabama. This settlement was called *Ochiapofa*: *ochi*, "hickory," *api*, "stem," "trunk," and *-ofa*, a locative suffix—literally "in the hickory grove."

If *Ocheesee* is of Hitchiti origin, then the word signifies "people of a different speech," from Hitchiti *ochisi*.

OCHLOCKONEE. 1. A bay on the coast of Franklin and Wakulla counties, an inlet of Apalachee Bay. 2. A river, rising in Worth County, Georgia, flowing southward through Georgia, and following in Florida the eastern boundary line of Gadsden and Liberty counties; then entering Franklin County and falling into Ochlockonee Bay. 3. A station on the Seaboard Air Line, in Leon County; mentioned by Lanier (1876), p. 328, as a small settlement in Wakulla County.

The name of the river has appeared in divers forms. Here are some of them:

    1733. APALACTHE or OGELAGANA, Popple Map.

    1755. APALACHEE or OGELAGANA. Mitchell Map.

    1818. OKE-LOCK-ONNE. Early Map of Georgia.

    1840. OCKLOCKONNEE R. Mackay and Blake.

    1856. OKLOKONEE R. Davis Map.

    1892. OKLOKONEE R. Norton's *Hdb*[3], Map.

    1899. OCKLOCKNEE R. Century Atlas of Fla.

    1931. OCHLOCKONEE R. Rand McNally Map.

This name is derived from Hitchiti *oki*, "water" and *lakni*, "yellow"—"yellow water." There is no authority for the translation "crooked."

OCHOPE. A hamlet in Collier County. The name signifies "field," according to information furnished me by Mr. J. L. Glenn, who is in charge of the Seminole Agency at Dania. He gives me the Seminole word as *ochupi*, with the primary stress on the final syllable.

The name *Ochope* is, I venture to suggest, rather a derivative of Sem.-Cr. *ochi-àpi*, "hickory tree," than of any other Seminole word. A former Upper Creek town, on the east bank of the Coosa River, about two miles above the fork, was called *Ochiapofa,* "in the hickory grove," and recorded as *Ocheubofau* or *Hickory Ground,* on the Early Map of Georgia, 1818. One of the Creek clans, too, is known as *Ochiàlgi,* "hickory nut clan."[21] Nevertheless, it is possible that Mr. Glenn's translation is correct; in that case, however, *Ochope* is a corruption of Sem.-Cr. *chapofa,* "field."

OCTAHATCHEE. A village in the northwestern corner of Hamilton County.

> 1892. OCTAHATCHEE. Norton, *op. cit.,* p. 33.

The name is derived from Sem.-Cr. *oktahàchi,* "sand creek," a syncopated form of *oktahà,* "sand," and *hàchi,* "creek."

OJUS. A town with a population of 558, on the Florida East Coast Railroad, in Dade County.

> 1930. OJUS. Sectional Map.

Seminole *ojas,* a derivative of Sem.-Cr. *ochità,* "to have," signifies "plentiful," the term apparently referring to the luxurious vegetation in the vicinity of the town.

OKAHUMPKA. A town with a population of 530, on the Atlantic Coast Line, in Lake County. As early as 1813 Okehumpkee was known to be a Seminole settlement; in 1823 its chief was Micanopy; in 1836 it was abandoned by the Seminoles.

> 1839. OKEEHUMKY. Taylor War Map.

> 1892. OKAHUMPKA. Norton, *op. cit.,* p. 46.

Norton, *op. cit.,* p. 376, translates *Okahumpka* by "bad water," apparently connecting the name with Hitchiti *oki,* "water," and *hampi,* "bad." This translation is erroneous not only because all the early spellings have *k,* but also because *k* could not possibly have arisen as a glide in such a form as *hampi.* Perhaps Hodge is right in translating the name by "lonely water," evidently taking it for a compound of Hitchiti *oki,* "water," and Cr.-Sem. *hàmki,* "one," "a certain."[22]

---

[21] Swanton, *BAE,* Rep. 42: 115.

[22] Hodge, *op. cit.,* 2: 114.

It is also possible that the name is connected with Hitchiti *oki,* "water," and Sem.-Cr. *homàki,* "bitter." The sand in the vicinity of Okahumpka is said to contain traces of tannic acid.

In the accepted spelling of *Okahumpka, p* represents a glide between *m* and *k.*

OKALOACOOCHEE SLOUGH. A swamp situated partly in Hendry and partly in Collier County.

Early spellings are *Oc-hol-wa-coochee,* Sprague, *op. cit.,* 1841, p. 300, and Sprague's map, *Ok-hol-oa-coochee.* The name signifies "little bad water," being derived from Hitchiti *oki,* "water," Creek *holwaki,* "bad," and Creek *-uchi,* "little."

This name must not be confused with *Oklawaha, q. v., infra,* the designation of a river situated much farther north, chiefly in Marion County.

OKALOO. A station on the Louisville Nashville Railroad, in the northern part of Oskaloosa County.

1930. OKALOO. Sectional Map.

The name seems to be the result of a shortening of *Okaloosa, q. v., infra.*

OKALOOSA. A county in the northwestern part of the State, formed in 1915 from Santa Rosa and Walton Counties.

The source of this name is Choctaw *oka,* "water," and *lusa,* "black"—"black water." This was also the name of a former Choctaw settlement or settlements, on Blackwater Creek, in Kemper County, Mississippi. There was another settlement, probably bearing the same name, on White's Branch, in the same county.

OKEECHOBEE. 1. A lake, approximately forty by twenty-five miles, in the southern part of the State.

1839. LAKE O-KEE-CHO-BEE or BIG WATER. Taylor Map.

According to Fontanedo this body of water was known to the Indians as *Lake Mayaimi* because of its large size. Cf. *Maimi, supra.* 2. A county, created in 1917, with a population of 4,129. 3. A town with a population of 1,797, situated in Okeechobee County, on the Florida East Coast Railway and the Seaboard Air Line.

Okeechobee is derived from Hitchiti *oki*, "water," and *chobi*, "big," the term "big water" being applied indiscriminately to brooks, small streams, and large bodies of water.

OKEELANTA.　A hamlet on the North New River Canal, *mail* South Bay, several miles south of Lake Okeechobee, in Palm Beach County.

　　1930.　OKEELANTA.　Sectional Map.

The name is said to be composed of Hitchiti *oki*, "water," and *lanta*, apparently a pseudo-Latin designation of the Atlantic Ocean, I am informed by Miss Maud Hartline, of South Bay.

OKEFENOKEE.　An extensive swamp, covering an area of nearly 700 square miles, in southeastern Georgia and the adjoining part of northern Florida.

　　1839.　OKEFINOKEE SWAMP.　Taylor War Map.
　　1840.　OKIFINOKEE SWAMP.　Mackay Blake Map
　　　　　of East Florida.
　　1892.　OKEFENOKEE SWAMP.　Map in Norton's
　　　　　Florida.

This name, which signifies "shaking water," is derived from Hitchiti *oki*, "water," and *finoki*, "shaking."

OKHAKONKONHEE.　A lake in Polk County, southwest of Lake Kissimee.

On my copy of the Davis Map, 1856, the name is recorded as *Okhakonkonhee*, whereas in Hodge's *Handbook*, II, 104, under *Oclackonayahe*, the lake is called *Okliakonkonhee*. If the Davis map records the more primitive form, I am disposed to interpret the name —though with great hesitancy—as a corruption of Creek *akhauke*, "mudhole," and *kunhi*, "crooked"— that is, a crooked lake with many mudholes. If, however, Hodge's form is nearer the original source, then I take the name to be a compound of Hitchiti *oki*, "water," Sem.-Cr. *làko*, "big," and Sem.-Cr. *kunhi*, "crooked"—"crooked big water." In the second source for the name, Hitchiti *oki* is to be regarded as a loanword in the Seminole-Creek dialect. The present name of the lake—*Crooked Lake*—dates from about 1883. "Crooked" is *kutukbi* in Hitchiti.

Whatever the correct analysis of the name may be, the last two syllables certainly correspond to Sem.-Cr. *kunhi,* "crooked." On the map that accompanies Norton's *Handbook,* the name has, in fact, been simplified to "Crooked L."

It may be just as well to note here the meaning of *Oclackonayahe,* which was the name of a former Seminole settlement (1822) on or near the lake in Polk County. I believe the name to be a derivative of the Hitchiti loan-word *oki,* "water," Sem.-Cr. *làko,* "big," and Sem.-Cr. *yànahi,* "crooked"—"crooked big water."

OKLAWAHA. 1. A river which flows in a northerly direction through Marion County, and thence turns eastward to empty into the St. Johns River, twenty-five miles south of Palatka.

> 1839. OCKLAWAHA RIVER. Taylor War Map.
> 1930. OCKLAWAHA R. Sectional Map.

2. A creek, an affluent of the Ochlockonee River, in Gadsden County.

Sprague, *op. cit.,* p. 252, translates *Ocklawaha* by "bad crossing"; Rhodes and Dumont, in their *Guide to Florida,* p. 233, by "dark crooked river." The name is derived from Sem.-Cr. *aklowahi,* "muddy," "boggy."

OLUSTEE. 1. A creek forming the boundary between Columbia and Union counties and emptying into the Santa Fe River. 2. A town of 1,355 inhabitants, on the Seaboard Air Line, in Baker County.

> 1839. OULUSTA CR. Taylor War Map.
> 1856. OLUSTEE C. Davis Map.
> 1856. OLUSTEE (village). Davis Map.
> 1931. OLUSTEE (creek and village). Rand McNally Map.

At Olustee, on February 20, 1864, the Confederates defeated the Union forces in a severe engagement in which the losses on both sides were heavy. (Norton, *op. cit.,* pp. 333 ff.)

Olustee is corrupted from Sem.-Cr. *oklàsti,* "blackish."

ONOSHAHATCHEE. A stream falling into Alligator Bay about two miles southeast of Possum Key, I am informed by Mr. C. S. Smallwood, of Chokoloskee.

Onoshahatchee is evidently corrupted from Sem.-Cr. *osànà,* "otter," and *hàchi,* "creek," or "river."

OPA LOCKA. A village with a population of 339, on the Seaboard Air Line, in Dade County. The name was selected by Mr. Glenn H. Curtis.

Opa Locka refers to a hammock situated within the present limits of the village. The source is Seminole *opilwa*, "swamp," and *làko*, "big," though this combination appears in most cases as *opillako*. Moore-Wilson's rendition of the name by "west," in *The Seminoles of Florida,* p. 121, rests on a misapprehension of Seminole *akalatkà*, "west."

OSCEOLA. 1. A village of comparatively recent origin, with a population of 310, on the Florida East Coast Railroad, in Seminole County. 2. A county formed in 1887 from Brevard and Orange Counties.

Osceola, the most noted of all the Seminole chiefs, was born on the Tallapoosa River, in the Creek country, about 1803. He led his people against the forces of the United States at the beginning of the Seminole War; but, after defeating or baffling several expeditions sent against him, he was treacherously seized on October 12, 1837, under a flag of truce, by order of General Thomas S. Jesup. Osceola died in January, 1838, a prisoner at Fort Moultrie, South Carolina, to which he had been removed from Castle St. Marco, now Fort Marion, St. Augustine.

Osceola is derived from Creek *àsi-yahola*, "black drink hallooer." Creek *àsi* signifies "leaves," and designates specifically the leaves of the Yaupon *(Ilex Cassine* Walt. 1788, or *Ilex Vormitoria* Ait.), from which the Indians of the Gulf Coast formerly prepared a famous black drink for use on all festive and ceremonial occasions.

The second element in *Osceola* is *yahola*, a term found in many war titles, such as *yahola fiksiko*, "heartless yahola," and *yahola hajo*, "mad yahola." The term *yahola* signifies the cry uttered by the attendants while the chiefs were sipping the black drink, and also designates a powerful male deity whose call was like the yahola note.[23]

---

[23] See Gatschet, *op. cit.,* 1: 177-183; 2: 80, 142; Swanton, *BAE,* Rep. 42: 485, 565, 666; and the present writer's *Louisiana-French,* under *Cassinier,* pp. 84-86.

OSKIN. A station on the Louisville and Nashville Railway in Okaloosa County.

> *Oskin* is the objective case of Sem.-Cr. *oski*, "rain." The name is of recent application.

OSOWAW. A station on the Florida East Coast Railroad, in the northeastern corner of Okeechobee County.

> *Osowaw*, a name of recent application, is corrupted from Sem.-Cr. *osahwà*, "crow." This name does not signify "bird," which in Seminole-Creek is *fuswa* or *fus*, the latter being usually found in compounds, as in *fus fiksiko*, "heartless bird," and *fus hajo*, "mad bird."

OTAHITE. A hamlet near the western boundary of Okaloosa County.

> 1892. OTAHITE. Norton, *op. cit.*, p. 88.
>
> 1930. OTAHITE. Sectional Map.

> This name seems to be intended for Seminole *otohità*, "to be damp."

> Or is *Otahite* a variant of *Otaheite*, the former designation of *Tahiti*, the largest of the French Society Islands in the South Pacific? The word has become popular through its use in such terms as the *Otaheite apple* and the *Otaheite orange*.

> The name *Tahiti* is apparently related to *tahe*, which in Tahiti and some other Polynesian dialects signifies "to flow." Compare Paumotu *tahe*, "river," and *taheta*, "spring," "fountain," the latter belonging to the Rapanui dialect of Easter Island.[24]

PAHOKEE. A town of 2,256 inhabitants, situated on the southeastern shore of Lake Okeechobee, in Palm Beach County.

> 1930. PAHOKEE. Sectional Map.

> This name is composed of Hitchiti *pàhi*, "grass," and *oki*, "water"—"grass water"—a term applied by the Seminoles to the Everglades, a vast expanse of shallow water, covering an area of perhaps 5,000 square miles and overgrown with reeds and saw grass (*Cladium effusum* Torr.). Lying to the south and east of Okeechobee Lake, and attaining a maximum width of approxi-

---

[24] See William Churchill, *Easter Island*, p. 264.

mately fifty miles, this extensive sea of grass is intersected by narrow channels and dotted with numerous small islands. On the Taylor War Map, 1839, the name of the Everglades is recorded as *Pay-hai-o-kee or Grass Water*.

PALATKA. 1. A town with a population of 6,500, on the Atlantic Coast Line, and the west bank of the St. Johns River, in Putnam County. 2. East Palatka, a village with 387 inhabitants, just across the river from Palatka.

> 1830. PILATKI. Taylor Map.
> 1840. PILATKA. Mackay and Blake Map.
> 1846. PALATKA. Sprague, *op. cit.*, pp. 256, 306, and often.
> 1870. PILATKA. Colton Map.
> 1892. PALATKA, and East Palatka. Norton, *op. cit.*, p. 81.

Pilatka was originally a town, no doubt Seminole, on or near the site of the present Palatka. Jacksonville, Florida, is said to have been known as *waca pilatka*, a term that has been interpreted as "cows' crossing," whence its former English name of "Cows' Ford."

Pilatka is shortened and corrupted, in my opinion, from Sem.-Cr. *pilotaikità*, "a ferry," which is composed in turn of Sem. *pilo*, "boat," and *taikità*, "ford," "crossing." Compare the Choctaw term for "ferry"—*peni intalaia*, which is literally *peni*, "boat," *in*, "its," and *talaia*, "trail."

PALATLAKAHA. A creek emptying into Lake Harris, in Lake County. This spelling is recorded on Norton's map of Lake County, *op. cit.*, p. 46. The form *Falatlakaha*, shown on the Sectional Map of the Department of Agriculture, 1930, is manifestly erroneous.

Palatlakaha is corrupted, I am sure, from *Pilaklikaha*, the name of a hammock and an ancient settlement, possibly Negro, situated in Sumter County near the site of Dade's battle ground. The massacre of Dade's command took place December 28, 1835.

Pilaklikaha is recorded on the Taylor War Map of 1839.

Pilaklikaha signifies "big swamp site," the elements of the name being *opilwa*, "swamp," *làko*, "big," and *laiki*, "site." For the variant spelling of the name, see

Hodge, *op. cit.*, 2: 249. I may note here that whereas Sprague, *op. cit.*, p. 465, refers to the Palacklikaha hammock, he uses, on pages 460 and 462, the spelling *Palaklakaha*.

PANASOFFKEE. 1. A lake in Sumter County. 2. A village of 189 inhabitants at the southern extremity of the lake, on the Seaboard Air Line.

> 1839. PANEESUFEKEE LAKE. Taylor Map.
> 1856. PANASOFKEE L. Davis Map.
> 1892. L. PANASOFFKE; Panasoffkee village, Norton, p. 86.

Panasoffkee is a derivative of Sem. *pani*, "valley," and *sufki*, "deep"—"deep valley."

PEACE CREEK. A stream emptying into Charlotte Harbor, on the West Coast of Florida.

On the map of America (1527) by Hernando Colon there is, on the west coast of Florida, an unnamed bay at the head of which stands the name "R de la paz." In Oviedo's history, published from 1535 to 1555, there is in Vol. II, p. 144, the phrase "Sur el rio de la Paz." Jacobus Lemoyne's map has "F. Pacis." The original name, then, was "Peace River."[25]

That the Seminoles, however, thought of this stream as "Peas Creek" becomes clear from the designation "Talakchopko or Pease Cr.," on the Taylor War Map, 1839. In Seminole *tàlako* is the word for "pea," and *chàpko* signifies "long"—hence "cow-peas," "black-eyed peas," literally, "long peas." Indeed, Gaffarel, on his *Carte de la Floride (1562-1568)*, designates the stream by the name "Pease."

PENNICHAW. A station on the Florida East Coast Railroad, *mail* Maytown, in Volusia County, recorded on the Sectional Map, 1930.

Pennichaw is Seminole for "turkey gobbler" according to Moore-Wilson, *op. cit.*, p. 118. The first part of the name is taken from Sem.-Cr. *pinwà*, "turkey," but the rest of the name is not perfectly clear to me. I am disposed to connect the name with Seminole *pinhàchi*, "turkey tail," or perhaps with *pin hajo*, "mad turkey," a busk and war title.

---

[25] Cf. Lowery, *op. cit.*, 1: 442, 445.

PENSACOLA. 1. A city of 31,579 inhabitants, in Escambia County. 2. A bay on which the city is located.

    1699. PENSACOLAS. Pénicaut, in French, *Hist. Coll. La.*, n. s., I (1869), 38.

    1701. PANSACOLAS. Gravier, in Shea, *Early Voy.* (1861), p. 159.

    1723. PENÇOCOLOS. Barcia, *Ensayo*, p. 316.

    1733. PENSACOLA. Popple Map.

    1741. PENSICOLA. Coxe, *Carolana*, p. 28.[26]

Pensacola is a derivative of Choctaw *panshi*, "hair," and *okla*, "people," a name conferred on the Pensacola Indians because the men as well as the women wore their hair long.

The Pensacola, a Muskhogean tribe, once occupied the region about the present city and harbor of Pensacola.

PITHLACHASCOTEE. A river emptying into the Gulf at New Port Richey, Pasco County.

    1839. PITHLOCHASCOTEE R. Taylor Map.

    1856. PITHLOCHASCOTEE R. Davis Map.

    1892. PITHLACHASCOTEE R. Norton, p. 75.

According to Mr. Gerben de Vries, postmaster at New Port Richey, this stream is known locally as the "Cootee."

The source of this name is Sem.-Cr. *pilo*, "canoe," and *chàskita*, "to chop," "to cut"—that is to say, "the river where canoes are made."

PITHLACHOCCO. A lake in Alachua county; also called *Newnan's Lake*, after Colonel Newnan, a Georgia volunteer in the Seminole War.

    1839. PITHLOCHOCO LAKE. Taylor Map.

    1856. PITHLACHOCCO. Davis Map.

The source is Sem. *pilo*, "boat," and *chuko*, "house" —that is, a "ship," literally "boat house."

POCATAW. A station on the Florida East Coast Railroad, in Orange County; recorded on the map in Nevin O. Winter's *Florida* (Boston, 1918).

The origin of this name is Sem.-Cr. *pokta*, "twins."

---

[26] Cf. Hodge, *op. cit.*, 2: 227.

PORT MAYACA. A village of one hundred inhabitants, on the Florida East Coast Railroad, in the southwestern corner of Martin County.

The ancient Mayaca, a Timucua town, was situated several miles north of Cape Canaveral, on the St. Johns River, according to Fontanedo, whose account was written in Spain about 1575.[27]

The site of this town is clearly shown on a map of 1715 and also on the Popple map of 1733;[28] on both maps the name is recorded as *Mayaco*.

Mayaca, a variant of *Myakka* and *Miakka*, is thought to have the same meaning as *Miami, q. v., supra.*

SALOFKA. A station on the Florida East Coast Line, in Osceola County.

1930. SALOFKA. Sectional Map.

This name reproduces Seminole *islafkà*, "knife."

SEMINOLE. 1. A village of 155 inhabitants, on the Seaboard Air Line, in Pinellas County. Norton, *op. cit.*, p. 37, records this place-name. 2. Seminole Hills, a village of 250 inhabitants, in the western part of Bay County; a place-name of recent origin. 3. A county formed in 1913 from Orange County.

The name *Seminole*, from Creek *siminole*, "separatist," is applied to a Muskhogean tribe of Florida, consisting at first of immigrants for the most part from the Hitchiti, the Oconee, and the Mikasuki tribes of the Hitchiti linguistic group of Alabama or southern Georgia. The first Seminoles arrived in Florida about 1750, under Chief Secoffee. Later, in the second half of the eighteenth century, these were joined by contingents from the Alabama group and the Muskogee branch of the Muskhogean stock.

During the first quarter of the nineteenth century, the Creek or Muskogee immigrants to Florida became so numerous that they soon outnumbered every other Indian element among the Seminoles, and hence made the Seminole dialect virtually identical with the Creek. It is not surprising, therefore, to find that most of the Indian geographic names in Florida are of Creek, or Seminole-Creek, origin; that a much smaller number are

---

[27] Cf. Lowery, *op. cit.*, 1: 431.

[28] Swanton, *BAE*, Bul. 73, plate 4.

from the Hitchiti, which is nearly the same as the Mikasuki; that a few are formed by a union of Creek and
Hitchiti forms; and finally, that several names are met
with which have sprung from the Choctaw, a dialect
closely resembling the Chickasaw, but varying sharply
from the Creek and Hitchiti. Some Choctaw scouts are
known to have been with the American army in its con-
flicts with the Seminoles of Florida.

The Yuchi, a tribe probably identical with the Tama-
hita, are represented by *Euchee* and *Eucheeanna*, geographic names in Walton County, one of which is clearly
a coinage of white settlers. Indeed, the town, *Eucheeanna*, was founded by Scotch and Irish immigrants.

Some Yamasee bands, whose early history is connected with that of South Carolina, emigrated to Florida
and became absorbed there by larger bodies of Indians.
Compare the remarks on the name *Iamonia*, *supra*.

On April 1, 1932, the total number of Seminoles at
the Seminole Agency and Seminole Reservation in Florida was 562.

SOPCHOPPY. 1. A town of 1,188 inhabitants, on the
Seaboard Air Line, in Wakulla County. 2. A river in
the same county.

The name *Sopchoppy* has been corrupted from *Lock-
choppee*, the former designation of the stream in Wau-
kulla County.

      1856. LOCKCHOPPEE R. Davis Map.

      1870. SOPCHOPPY CR. Colton Map.

      1870. SOCKCHOPPY SETTLEMENT. Colton Map.

      1892. SOPCHOPPY: RIVER AND SETTLEMENT. Nor-
ton, p. 98.

      1931. SOPCHOPPY. Sectional Map.

Sem.-Cr. *lokchàpi* signifies the (red) oak; the word
is composed of *lokcha*, "acorn," and *àpi*, "stem."

STEINHATCHEE. 1. A river in the counties of Lafayette
and Dixie.

      1839. ESTEEN-HATCHEE RIVER. Taylor Map.

      1870. STEINHATCHEE R. Colton Map.

2. A town with a population of 322, in Dixie County,
recorded by *The Century Atlas*, 1899.

The word signifies "man's river," from *isti*, "man,"
in, "his," and *hàchi*, "river." Sprague, in his *Florida*

War, p. 252, gives the name as *Esteen-Hatchee,* and the translation as "Man River." It may be significant that this stream falls into Deadman's Bay.

STILLIPICA.   A settlement in Madison County, just east of the present Moseley Hall.   The settlement seems to have been abandoned.

> 1870. STILLEPICA. Colton Map.
>
> 1892. STILLIPICA. Norton Map.

This name is derived from Sem.-Cr. *(i)stilipaika,* "moccasin," "shoe," a word that is composed of *isti,* "person," *ili,* "foot," and *àpaiki,* "within"—"some one's foot within."

TALLAHASSEE.   A city, the capital of Florida, with a population of 10,700, situated on the Seaboard Air Line, in Leon County.   A Seminole town formerly occupied the site of the present Tallahassee.   In 1799 Hawkins calls the town *Sim-e-no-le-tallau-haf-see,* a name in which *f* has the value of *s.*[29]

In 1792 William Bartram had visited the town and found it to consist of about thirty houses.

Tallahassee is a derivative of Creek *tàlwa,* "town," and *hasi,* "old"—hence "old town."

TALOFA.   A hamlet in Putnam County; recorded in the Index of the Rand McNally Map, 1931.   Sem.-Cr. *tàlofà* signifies "town," "tribe," "settlement."

TALUGA.   A river, a tributary of the Ochlockonee, in Liberty County.

> 1839. TALUGIA RIVER. Taylor Map.
>
> 1850. TALUGA R. Davis Map.

This name seems to be shortened and corrupted from Sem. *tàlako chàpko,* "cow peas."

In 1799 Hawkins gives *Tal-lau-gue chapco pop-cau,* "a place where cowpeas are eaten," as the name of a Seminole town.[30]   It is also significant that Pease Creek —now Peace Creek, according to the United States Geographic Board—was designated *tàlako chàpko,* by the Seminoles; cf. *Peace Creek, supra.*

---

[29] *Georgia Historical Society Coll.,* 3: 25.

[30] *Georgia Hist. Soc. Coll.,* 3: 25.

Sem.-Cr. *tàlako,* "peas," or "beans," without the addition of the adjective *chàpko,* "long," may be, of course, the source of the name. See *Telogia, infra.*

TAMPA. An ancient Calusa town on the southwest coast of Florida, described by Fontanedo in 1565 as a large town. Its name was bestowed on a bay, which is recorded as "B. de Tampa" on a map entitled *Insulae Americanae in Oceano Septentrionali* (c. 1671).[31]

Tampa Bay is shown on the Taylor War Map of 1839, and later maps.

The population of the present city of Tampa, in Hillsborough County, is estimated at 101,161.

Tampa Downs and Tampa Northern Junction are stations on the Seaboard Air Line, in Hillsborough County. Tampashores, with a population of 280, is on the same railroad, in Pinellas County. Port Tampa and Port Tampa City, the latter with 1,242 inhabitants, are on the Atlantic Coast Line, in Hillsborough County. Tampa Bay Hotel is a station, near Tampa, on the Atlantic Coast Line. The Tamiami Trail is a highway that extends across the Everglades and connects Tampa with Miami; hence the modern name *Tamiami,* which has also been given to a station on the Seaboard Air Line, in Lee County.

The name *Tampa* is a corruption of Creek *itimpi,* "near it."

TELOGIA. A town of 476 inhabitants, on the Apalachicola Northern Railway, in Liberty County.

Telogia, which is recorded by the Sectional Map, 1930, is apparently a corruption of *Taluga, q. v., supra. Taluga* is spelled *Tologie,* in Sidney Lanier's *Florida* (1876), p. 334.

THONOTOSASSA. 1. A lake in Hillsborough County, northeast of Tampa. 2. A town with a population of 896, on the Atlantic Coast Line, in the same county.

　　　1839. LAKE THLONOTOSASSA. Taylor Map.
　　　1892. THONOTOSASSA LAKE. Norton, *op. cit.,* p. 37.
　　　1892. THONOTOSASSA TOWN. Norton, p. 37.
　　　1930. THONOTOSASSA or LAKE OF FLINTS. Sectional Map.

---

[31] Cf. Brinton, *op. cit.,* p. 115, footnote 2.

This name is derived from Sem.-Cr. *lonoto*, "flint," and *sasi*, "is there." The voiceless *l* of Sem.-Cr. *lonoto* is indicated in the spelling of 1839 by *Thl-*.

TOHOPKEE. A station on the Florida East Coast Railroad, in Osceola County. Like most other railway stations of Indian origin, *Tohopkee* is of comparatively recent application. The source is Sem.-Cr. *tohopki*, "fort."

TOHOPEKALIGA AND EAST TOHOPEKALIGA. Lakes in the northern part of Osceola County.

> 1839. LAKE TOHOPEKALIGA. Taylor Map.
>
> 1892. EAST TOHOPEKALIGA L., Tohopekaliga L. Norton, p. 72.

The name signifies "the site of a fort," from Sem.-Cr. *tohopki*, "fort," and *laiki*, "site," an abstract noun formed from *laikita*, "to sit."

TOMOKA. A creek in Volusia County.

> 1839. TOMOKA R. Taylor Map.
>
> 1856. TOMOKA CR. Davis Map.

Tomoka is a variant spelling of *Timucua*, the name of the largest of all the Indian tribes that formerly inhabited Florida. The Timucuan family embraces a group of cognate tribes that occupied the greater part of northern Florida, their domain extending, on the east coast, from near the present site of Malabar to a point beyond the mouth of St. Johns River, and, on the west coast, from Tampa Bay northward as far as Aucilla River, which flows along the northwestern boundary of Taylor County. The Timucua tribe, whose name designates the group of kindred tribes, occupied the region about Santa Fe Lake, in Alachua County, and extended their authority to the eastern shore of the St. Johns River. One of the Timucuan villages, which the French named *Timogoa*, is said to signify "lord," "ruler," and to be a compound of *atimuca*, "waited upon (*muca*) by servants (*ati*)." Some other spellings of the name are *Timucua, Timoqua, Timuca, Tymangona, Tymangona, Thimogona, Thimogoa, Thimagou, Timogona, Timoga, Tomoco,* and *Atimaco*. The last two forms are English.[32]

---

[32] See Hodge, *op. cit.*, 2: 752-754; Gatschet, *op. cit.*, 1: 12; Lowery, *op. cit.*, 2: 407-409.

TOTOSAHATCHEE. A stream that enters the St. Johns River just south of the village called *Christmas,* in the present Orange County.

    1839. TO-TO-LOSE HATCHEE. Taylor Map.

    Sem.-Cr. *totolosi* is "chicken," and *hàchi* is "creek." This stream is now called *Totosahatchee Creek,* according to Miss Juanita S. Tucker, of Christmas, Florida.

TSALA APOPKA LAKE. A body of water in Citrus County.

    1856. L. CHARLEY APOPKA. Davis Map.

    1870. LAKE CHARLEY APAPKA. Colton Map.

    1892. TSALA APAPKA L. Norton, p. 13.

    The source of this name is Sem.-Cr. *chalo,* "trout," and *papka,* "eating place"—"the lake where trout are eaten." Cf. *Charley Apopka, supra.*

WACAHOOTA. A station on the Jacksonville, Gainesville and Gulf Railroad, in Alachua County.

    1839. WATKAHOOTEE FORT. Taylor Map.

    1841. WACAHOOTA. Sprague, *op. cit.,* p. 307.

    1856. WACAHOTEE. Davis Map.

    1870. WACAHOTIE. Colton Map.

    1930. WACAHOOTA. Sectional Map.

    The modern railroad station lies farther to the northwest than the *Wacahotee* of the Davis Map and the *Wacahotie* of the Colton Map.

    The name signifies "cow barn," the source being Creek *waka,* "cow," and *huti,* "home." *Waca* is an adaptation of Spanish *vaca,* "cow."

WACO. A hamlet in Madison County: recorded on the Sectional Map of Florida, 1930.

    Waco may be the Seminole *wako,* "little blue heron" (*Florida caerulea caerulea* L.), or it may be a reminiscence of the well-known Texas place-name, which is apparently a shortened form of the tribal designation *Tawakoni,* "river bend among red sand hills." My correspondents, unfortunately, have no idea who selected this name.

WACASASSA. A river flowing southward through Levy County, to empty into Wacasassa Bay, about twelve miles east of Cedar Key.

1839. WACASSA RIVER. Taylor Map.

1856. WACASASSA R.; WACASASSA BAY. Davis Map.

The name was conferred on the stream and bay because their banks were frequented by herds of cattle. *Wacasassa* signifies "cattle range," being derived from Sem.-Cr. *waka*, "cattle," and *sasi*, "there are." *Waca* is from Spanish *vaca*, "cow."

WAHOO. A village in Sumter County, recorded on the Sectional Map, 1930.

On November 21, 1836, the United States troops, under the command of Colonel Pierce, compelled a large force of Indians to retreat into the Wahoo Swamp, which lies near the present Wahoo.

Wahoo is derived from Creek *uhawhu*, which designates (1) the Winged Elm *(Ulmus alata* Michx.), (2) the White Basswood *(Tilia heterophylla* Vent.). The latter tree has various other names: *bee-tree, linden, white linn, teil-* or *tile-tree, cottonwood, silver leaf poplar,* and *wahoo.* The former tree is also called *wahoo, water elm, cork elm,* and *witch elm.*

WAKULLA. 1. A famous spring fifteen miles south of Tallahassee.

1856. WAKULLA SPR. Davis Map.

2. A river which unites with the St. Marks and falls into Apalachee Bay.

1839. WAUCULLAH RIVER. Taylor Map.

3. A county formed from Leon County in 1843. 4. A town with 497 inhabitants, on the Seaboard Air Line, in Wakulla County: recorded by *The Century Atlas*, 1899.

This name is said to signify "mystery." If so, it may be composed of Sem.-Cr. *wiwa*, "water," and *àlahki*, "strange," with the loss of the initial syllable of *wiwa* and metathesis of the *k* and *l* in *àlahki*. I doubt seriously, however, whether this translation is correct. The name may be derived much more simply from *Wahkolà*, the Creek word for a loon, two species of which winter in Florida—*Gavia immer* (Brunn.) and the red-throated loon *(Gavia stellata* Pont).

WAUKEENAH. A town with a population of 906, in Jefferson County.

1856. WAKEENA. Davis Map.

This is a perplexing name. Nevertheless, the spelling of 1856 points to Sem.-Cr. *waka,* "cow," and *ina,* "body"—a "cow's body"—as the probable source. A trivial incident, as is well known, is sometimes responsible for an Indian's coinage of a geographic name.

WEEKIWACHEE. A short river in Hernando County, falling into the Gulf at Bayport.

1839. WEEKIWACHEE R. Taylor Map.

1856. WEKIWACHEE R. Davis Map.

Wekiwachee signifies "little spring," being composed of Cr. *wikaiwà,* "spring," and *-chi,* "little."

WEEWAHIIACA. See *Crystal River, supra.*

WEHAMBA. A creek flowing from Lake Walden, about a mile and a quarter southwest of Plant City, Hillsborough County, and falling into Thonotosassa Lake, which empties into the Hillsborough River, about sixteen miles northeast of Tampa.

1913. WEHAMBA CREEK. Geologic and Topographic Map of Florida (Wash., 1913).

This creek is also known locally as *Pendleton Creek,* and appears on some maps of Hillsborough County as *Wehamta.*

This name is a derivative of Sem.-Cr. *wi-,* "water," and Hitchiti *hampi,* "bad"—"bad water."

WEKIWA. 1. A settlement near the northern boundary line of Orange County.

1930. WEKIWA. Sectional Map.

2. A creek emptying into the St. Johns River, in the southeastern corner of Lake County.

1839. WE-KI-WA CR. Taylor Map.

1892. WEKIWA CR. Norton, p. 68.

1930. WEKIWA CR. Sectional Map.

3. Wekiwa Springs, *mail* Apopka, Orange County: Index of Rand McNally Map, 1931.

The Seminoles are also said to have applied the name *Wikaiwa* to Blue Spring, situated twenty miles west of Ocala. The Spaniards called this spring *las Aguas Azules.*[33]

---

[33] Cf. Norton, *op. cit.,* p. 301.

A variant spelling, *Wekiva,* is sometimes found. Sem.-Cr. *wikaiwà* signifies a "spring of water."

WELAKA. A village of 409 inhabitants in Putnam County.

1870. WELAKA. Colton Map.

In 1876, Lanier refers to this place as a landing on the east bank of the St. Johns River, one hundred miles above Jacksonville.[34]

The Seminoles called the St. Johns River *Ylaco* or *Walaka.*[35] *Ylacco* seems to be intended for Cr. *wi-làko,* "river," or "big water," whereas *walaka* is a corruption of Cr. *wi-,* or *wiwa,* "water," and *alaka,* "coming"— hence "tide," "intermittent spring."

WEOHYAKAPKA. A lake in Polk County.

1839. LAKE WEEOK YAKAPKA. Taylor Map.

1856. WE SHYA KAPA L. Davis Map.

1892. WE-OH-YA-KAPKA L. Norton, p. 77.

1930. WALK IN THE WATER OR WEOHYAKAPKA L. Sectional Map.

This name is from the Sem.-Cr. *wi-,* "water," *oh,* "on," and *yàkàpaki,* "walking."

WETAPPO. A creek in Gulf County.

1856. WETAPPO CR. Davis Map.

The first part of this name is Cr. *wi-,* "water"; the second part is uncertain, but may be a corruption of Creek *tapho,* "broad"—hence "broad water."

On the Taylor War Map of 1839 there is a name that may throw light on the origin of *Wetappo;* this name is *Ar-chin-ner-ho Topho or Big Cypress,* the appellation of a tributary of the St. Johns River, situated just south of Wolf Creek, in the present Osceola and Brevard counties. *Ar-chin-ner-ho Topho* is clearly intended for Creek *àchinàho,* "cypress," and *tapho,* "broad," the alternative designation, *Big Cypress,* betraying a slightly inaccurate analysis of the Indian name; for "big" is *làko* in the Creek dialect. Returning now to *Wetappo,* I note that *tappo* and *tapho* sound very much alike in a rapid pronunciation.

[34] Sidney Lanier, *op. cit.,* p. 336.

[35] See Brinton, *op. cit.,* p. 154, footnote 1; and William Darby, *Memoir on the Geography,* etc., *of Florida* (Philadelphia, 1821), p. 85.

WETUMPKA. A town with a population of 742, in Gadsden County. *Wetumpka* is not very old; it is given by Norton, *op. cit.,* p. 31, in the form *Wetampha*—correctly as *Wetumpka, ibid.,* p. 391. There was apparently, however, a Seminole settlement of this name in the first half of the nineteenth century, near the present Emathla, in Marion County. Formerly the name also designated several Creek towns in Alabama, two of them in Elmore County, and a third in Russell County. The modern Wetumpka, in Alabama, occupies the site of one of these towns, about half a mile below Coosa Falls.

Wetumpka signifies "sounding water," or "tumbling water," the name being derived from Creek *wi-*, an abbreviation of *wiwa*, "water," and *tàmkà*, "sounding."

WEWAHITCHKA. A village of 584 inhabitants, near Dead Lake, in Gulf County. Norton, *op. cit.,* p. 12, records the name.

The source is Cr. *wiwa*, "water," and either *ahichka*, "view," or *ahichkità*, "to obtain"—hence "water view," or "the place where water was obtained."

WEWAHOTEE. A station on the Florida East Coast Railroad, in Orange County.

This is a modern name. Its source is *wiwa*, "water," and *huti*, "house"—that is, "water tank."

WHITEWATER BAY. A body of water situated in the southern end of Monroe County. The name is a translation of Sem.-Cr. *wi-* or *wiwa*, "water," and *hàtki*, "white," a term applied by the Seminoles and Creeks to the ocean.

WILLOCHOCHEE. A creek flowing from Decatur County, Georgia, into Gadsden County, Florida.

>1818. WE-THLUC-OO-CHEE. Early Map of Georgia.
>1892. WILLOCHOOCHEE. Norton, p. 31.
>1930. WILLOCHOCHEE. Sectional Map.

The spelling of 1818 corresponds to Creek *wi-lak-uchi*, a compound of *wi-*, "water," *làko*, "big," and *-uchi*, "little"—"little big water" or "little river." Cf. *Withlacoochee, infra.* The spellings of 1892 and 1930, on the other hand, point to the translation "little turtle water," being the equivalent of Sem.-Cr. *wi-*, "water," *locha,* "turtle," and *-uchi,* "little." These later spellings may be corrupt.

WIMICO. A lake and a river in Calhoun County.

> 1856. L. WIMICO. Davis Map.

> This name is derived from Sem.-*Cr. wi-*, "water," and *miko,* "chief"—"chief water."

WITHLA. A hamlet of 106 inhabitants, on the Seaboard Air Line, in the northern part of Polk County.

> *Withla,* a modern name, is clearly an abbreviation of *Withlacoochee, q. v., infra.*

WITHLACOOCHEE. 1. A river flowing through southern Georgia and uniting with the Suwannee, at Ellaville, in Madison County, Florida.

> 1839. WITHLACOSHE RIVER. Taylor Map.
> 1846. WITHLACOOCHEE (Big Water). Sprague, p. 252.
> 1856. WITHLACOOCHEE R. Davis Map.

2. An important river of middle western Florida, falling into the Gulf at Port Inglis, Levy County. Norton, *op. cit.,* p. 232, describes this river as a swift stream with rocky bottom, and high, wooded, picturesque banks.

> 1839. WITHLACOOCHEE RIVER. Taylor Map.
> 1856. WITHLOCKOOCHEE R. Davis Map.

> The early spellings of the name confirm the essential accuracy of the translation, "little great water," from Cr. *wi-*, "water," *làko,* "big," and *-uchi,* "little." But as Creek *wi-làko* is frequently the equivalent of "river," we may translate the name by "little river."

> The *-thl-* group in *Withlacoochee* represents an attempt to reproduce the sound of the Creek voiceless *l* in *làko.*

WOLF CREEK. A tributary of the St. Johns, in the northeastern part of Osceola County.

> On the Taylor War Map, 1839, this creek appears with its Indian name *Ya-ha Hatchee*—in Creek, *yahà,* "wolf," and *hàchi,* "creek."

YA-HA HATCHEE. See *Wolf Creek, supra.*

YAHALA.   A town of 458 inhabitants, on the Atlantic
Coast Line, in Lake County.

       1892.   YALAHA.   Norton, p. 46.

    Yalaha is the equivalent of Sem.-Cr. *yàlàha,* "orange."

YEEHAW.   A station of recent origin on the Florida East
Coast Railway, in Indian River County.

    Sem.-Cr. *yahà,* "wolf," is the source of the name.

2. FLORIDA NAMES OF DUBIOUS AND UNKNOWN ORIGIN

ALAFIA. A town of 391 inhabitants, situated on a river of the same name, in Hillsborough County.

Lanier (1876) mentions Alafia as a post office and small settlement on the river.[36]

    1839. ALAFIA RIVER. Taylor Map.

    1870. ALAFIA RIVER. Colton Map.

    1870. ALAFIA (SETTLEMENT). Colton Map.

Alafia, according to Hodge, was a small Seminole town (1836) near the river of the same name, whose inhabitants were probably led by one "Chief Alligator" during the Seminole War of 1835-1842.[37]

According to Sprague, however, certain mixed bands of Indians were located much farther north than Alafia —in fact, west of the Suwannee River—where they resided under the control of Chief Alligator and *Cotzarfixiko-chopko* (Mad Tiger)—literally *katchà*, "panther," *fiksiko*, "heartless," and *chàpko*, "long"—"long, heartless panther."[38]

Whether *Alafia* is Indian I consider very doubtful. The first two syllables, it is true, suggest Sem.-Cr. *àlà*, "buckeye"; but the rest of the name seems to have no equivalent in Seminole. The name may be Spanish *alafia*, the designation of species of the dogbane family *(Apocynaceae)*, some of which are found in Florida— for example, *amsonia* and *trachelospermum*.

ALAPAHA. A river flowing from Georgia through Hamilton County, Florida, and falling into the Suwannee. The Little Alapaha is a branch of the Alapaha, in the same county.

    1839. ALAPAHA RIVER. Taylor Map.

    1856. ELAPAHA RIVER. Davis Map.

In 1821 there was a Seminole settlement called *A-la-pa-ha talofa*, situated on the river in what is now Hamilton County. *Talofa* is Creek for "town," but *alapaha* is obscure. *Alapaha*, however, may have something to

---

[36] Lanier, *op. cit.*, p. 312.

[37] Cf. Hodge, *op. cit.*, 1: 35.

[38] Cf. Sprague, *op. cit.*, p. 272.

do with Creek *apala,* "on the other side," or with Creek *pàhi,* "grass." Compare also Hitchiti *alipi,* "up" (stream).

ASPALAGA. A steamboat landing on the east bank of the Apalachicola River, near Rock Bluff, Liberty County.

Aspalaga was a former Seminole settlement at or near the site of the present landing.

> 1839. ASPALAGA. Taylor Map.
>
> 1856. ASPALAGA. Davis Map.

The spelling *Aspalaga* occurs in 1680 as the name of a Spanish mission in the country of the Apalachee Indians, the full name of the mission being *San José de Ospalaga.*[39] On the Popple map of 1733 the Apalachee settlement is recorded as *Asapalaga,* and its site is fixed slightly east of the "Apalachee or Ogelagana R." Both *Apalachee* and *Ogelagana* are Hitchiti names, the former signifying "on the other side"—compare *Apalachicola, supra*—and the latter, "yellow water," from Hitchiti *oki,* "water," and *lakni,* "yellow."

I doubt whether it is possible to interpret the name *Aspalaga.* It bears a striking resemblance to *Yapalaga,* the designation of a town which was situated, according to the Popple map, in the vicinity of Asapalaga. The *Asapalaga* of the Popple map may be of Choctaw origin: compare Choctaw *osapa,* "cornfield," and *haloka,* "beloved." If the name is Hitchiti, its first element may have something to do with Hitchiti *aspi,* "corn," or with *àsi,* "yaupon leaves." *Àsi* is also a Creek word.

ASTATULA. 1. A lake about twelve miles long, in Lake County, originally called by the Indian name of *Astatula.* It is now known as *Lake Harris,* in honor of an early settler from Georgia. Lake Eustis, which is connected with Lake Harris, takes its name from that of a general in the United States army; and *Eustis* formerly followed *Astatula* as a designation of both bodies of water.

> 1839. LAKE EUSTIS. Taylor Map.
>
> 1856. LAKE EUSTIS. Davis Map.
>
> 1870. LAKE HARRIS. Colton Map.
>
> 1892. LAKE HARRIS OR ASTATULA. Norton, p. 46.

---

[39] Swanton, *BAE,* Bul. 73: 110, 323.

2. A village of 167 inhabitants, on the Tavares and Gulf Railroad, near the southern extremity of the lake. The village has received the name of the lake.

The word *Astatula* is said to signify "Lake of Sunbeams," or, according to some other natives of Florida, "Lake of Sparkling Moonbeams." Whatever the meaning of the name may be, there is certainly nothing in the Seminole dialect to justify either of these translations. The only suggestion, however, which I can offer is that *Astatula* is intended for Sem.-Cr. *isti,* "people," and *itàlwa,* "tribes"—"people of different tribes."[40]

AUCILLA. 1. A river forming the southeastern boundary of Jefferson County and flowing into Apalachee Bay. 2. A town of the same name with 982 inhabitants, situated on the Seaboard Air Line, in Jefferson County. This town is near the site of Fort Ocilla, which appears on the Taylor War Map of 1839. On the same map the name of the river is recorded as *Ocilla.*

In 1823 there was a Seminole town called *Oscillee* at the mouth of the river, on the east bank, in Taylor County. The chief of this town was Latafixico (Cr. *holahta fiksiko*), "heartless chief."

The name *Aucilla* is due to a reminiscence of an ancient Timucua town, which appears among early writers in such varied forms as *Assile, Agile, Axille, Aguil, Ochile, Ocilla,* and *Asile.* Its meaning is unknown.

CALOOSA. 1. A modern telegraph station in Lee County, *mail* Fort Myers. 2. CALOOSAHATCHEE. A river flowing from the vicinity of Lake Okeechobee, between Monroe and Manatee counties, and emptying into Charlotte Harbor, on the Gulf Coast. Bartram (1792) mentions a former Seminole town by the name of *Caloosahatche,* which was situated on this river.[41]

The Calusa were an important tribe, residing in South Florida, chiefly on what is now Charlotte Harbor and the Caloosahatchee River. In early French and Spanish records their name appears as *Calos, Carlos,* and *Caluça.* On January 3, 1541, Ranjel, for example, refers to Caluça as a place of much repute among the Indians; a province of more than ninety villages not

---

[40] Cf. Gatschet, *op. cit.,* 2: 121.

[41] William Bartram, *Travels,* p. 462.

subject to any one, with a savage population, very war-like and much dreaded.[42] The English corrupted the form *Carlos* to *Charlotte* (Harbor).

That the language of the Calusa, surviving now almost exclusively in a few place-names, shows affinity with Choctaw, seems to have been established by Swanton. The name *Caloosa*, for instance, may be a combination of Choctaw *kàllo*, "strong," and *lusa*, "black"; or of Choctaw *kàllo*, and *ansha*, "to be."[43] The second element in *Caloosahatchee* is Seminole *hàchi*, "river."

CHETOLAH. A station on the Florida East Coast Railroad, *mail* Jensen, in St. Lucie County.

> 1899. CHETOLAH. *Century Atlas.*

I connect this name very doubtfully with Choctaw *chitoli*, "loud," "hard," "large."

If the name is imported, it may be from *chitola*, "rattlesnake," the designation of a Zuñi clan.

CHIPOLA. 1. A river that flows southwest through Jackson County and empties into Chipola Lake in Calhoun County.

> 1856. CHIPOLA R. Davis Map.
>
> 1856. CHIPOLA L. Davis Map.

2. A station on the Marianna and Blountstown Railway in Calhoun County; recorded by Norton, *op. cit.*, p. 12.
3. A landing, *mail* Wewahitchka, in Calhoun County; recorded by Rand McNally, 1931.

I can think of no absolutely convincing etymology for *Chipola*. Perhaps the name is from Choctaw *chepulli*, "feast," "great dance," or represents a shortening of Creek *hàchapala*, "on the other side of the stream"—sometimes, "upstream." I consider the latter etymology the more plausible.

CHUMUCKLA. A small settlement of twenty-seven inhabitants situated in the western part of Santa Rosa County.

This place-name is not recorded on the Davis Map of 1856, nor is it mentioned in Sprague's *Seminole War* (1848), or in Lanier's *Florida* (1876).

---

[42] Bourne, *Narratives of De Soto*, 2: 132; Cf. also Hodge, *op. cit.*, 1: 195-196.
[43] Swanton, *BAE*, Bul. 73: 29-30.

The origin of *Chumuckla,* in spite of the late appearance of the name, is far from being clear. Creek *chumuklita,* indeed, which signifies "to bow the head to the ground," closely resembles *Chumuckla* in form; but the reason why a place-name of this peculiar meaning should have been selected is not apparent. The first syllable of *Chumuckla*—to suggest another interpretation—may possibly be connected with Hitchiti *ichi,* "deer," and the last two syllables with *imokli,* "its den"—hence "deer den," or "deer retreat."

COLEE. A small settlement on the east bank of the St. Johns River, in St. Johns County.

The name is modern and may not be Indian. One of my informants, indeed, writes that it is Indian for "cold." But Sem. *kàsàpi* signifies "cold." Sem. *itkolità,* "to have chills," or Sem. *kàlà,* "white oak," may be the source. Compare, however, the English family name *Coley.*

COLOHATCHEE. A station on the Florida East Coast Railroad and Seaboard Air Line, in Broward County; recorded on the map in Winter's *Florida.*

This name is probably composed of Sem.-Cr. *kàlà,* "white oak," and *hàchi,* "river," or "creek." According to another view the first element of *Colohatchee* is a corruption of (William) *Collier,* the name of an early settler.

ESCAMBIA. A river running between Escambia and Santa Rosa counties and falling into Escambia Bay. 2. Escambia Bay, an arm of Pensacola Bay. 3. A station on the Louisville and Nashville Railroad, in Escambia County.

On a part of the Purcell map, drawn about 1770, there is shown a *Branch of Scambia,* just south of the forks of the Coosa and Tallapoosa rivers, in Alabama. On an early map of Georgia, 1818, there appears the modern spelling of the name *Escambia,* the Escambia and the Little Escambia rivers being recorded as tributaries of the Connecuh ("crooked") River.

The name *Escambia* has been associated with Spanish *cambiar,* "to barter," "to exchange." This etymology I believe to be false. The name is probably Indian, though I cannot suggest for it a convincing etymology.

The ending of the name resembles the Choctaw or Chickasaw *àbi*, "killer," a popular suffix in war titles. Compare *Tuscumbia*, the name of a town in Colbert County, Alabama, which is probably derived from Choctaw or Chickasaw *tàshka*, "warrior," and *àbi*, "killer"— unless it be shortened from Chickasaw *tàshka umbàchi*, "warrior rainmaker." Whether Choctaw *ishkiàbi*, "a matricide," may be regarded as a plausible source of *Escambia*, I am unable to affirm. That *Escambia*, however, has sprung from some Indian dialect finds additional confirmation in the formal resemblance of the name to *Escampaba*, which the Indians conferred on the bay of Carlos, Florida, in honor of a Caloosa chief of that name, according to Velasco, *Geografía y Descripción Universal de las Indias* (1571-1574), Madrid, 1894, p. 164.[44]

ETONIAH. 1. A creek in the northern part of Putnam County. 2. Etonia(h), a lake in the western part of the same county.

    1839. IT-TUNWAH C. Taylor Map.

    1856. ETONIAH C. Davis Map.

    1870. ETONIA CR. Colton Map.

    1892. ETONIAH L. Norton Map, p. 81.

    1930. ETONIA L. Sectional Map.

In the vicinity of Etoniah Creek there was formerly a Seminole settlement called *Etanie*, of which Chicote Hajo ("mad," "crazy") was chief in 1823. *Chicote* is found in Creek *chukotàlgi*, a clan closely related to the toad clan—in Creek, *sopaktàlgi*.[45]

The Taylor Map, 1839, records the name *Ittun-i-ah Scrub*, just west of *It-tun-wah C.*

The postmaster at Palatka informs me that the old form of this name is thought to have been *Ekoniah*, and that he is familiar with three different translations of the name. They are: "crooked stream," "deer place," and "rough waters." To these may be added Norton's interpretation of the name—"palmetto scrub."[46]

If an early form with -*k*- is ever found, then the name can be derived from Creek *kunhi*, "crooked." The form *Etoniah*, on the other hand, resembles Creek *iton-*

[44] Cf. Lowery, *op. cit.*, 1: 445.

[45] See Gatschet, *op. cit.*, 1: 155.

[46] Norton, *op. cit.*, p. 376.

ita, "to shed hair," literally "to shed itself," a reflexive verb derived from *tonita,* "to cut off hair." What logical connection, if any, exists between *Etoniah* and *itonita,* it is impossible to say. In view of the form *Ittun-i-ah* of the Taylor War Map there remains the probability that the first element of the name is Cr. *ito,* "tree," and that the second is *niha,* "rosin." Compare the Creek term for "pine rosin"—*chuli niha.* Perhaps, finally, the word is derived from Choctaw *itànaha,* "gathered."

I should add that in the South "palmetto scrub" is a common designation of the dwarf palmetto (*Sabal Adansonii* Guerns.). But the Creek name for the palmetto, like the Choctaw, is *tala;* and as to the other translations of *Etoniah*—"crooked stream," "deer place," and "rough waters"—I can only conclude that they are alike in finding no support either in Creek or in Choctaw.

HYPOLUXO. A station on the Florida East Coast and Seaboard Air Line, in Palm Beach County; mentioned by Norton, *op. cit.,* (1892), p. 226.

If this is a genuine Indian name, it may be connected with Seminole *hàpo,* "mound," "heap," or "pile," and *poloksi,* "round," "circular." Shell mounds are numerous in Florida both on the Atlantic Coast and on the Gulf.

KANAPAHA. A station on the Seaboard Air Line, in Alachua County.

> 1839. KANAPAHAW, settlement northwest of Ft. Micanopy. Taylor Map.

> 1892. KANAPAHA, railroad station. Norton, p. 1.

Kanapaha seems to be composed of Sem.-Cr. *kunawà,* "bead," and *pàhi,* "grass." Bead grass has a spike which resembles a chain of beads. Other names for this grass (*Paspalum setaceum* Michx.) are *slender paspalum, beard grass,* and *pitchfork grass.*

Another derivation is possibly Sem.-Cr. *kunu* or *konip,* "skunk," and *pàhi,* "grass," though I do not know whether the Seminoles use this term or not. Skunk grass (*Eragrostis major* Host.) is an ill-smelling but

handsome grass, which is found in sandy soil nearly
throughout the United States. It is also called *candy-
grass, stink-grass, pungent meadow-grass,* and *strong-
scented love-grass.*

Owing to the complete lack of any local information
about *Kanapaha,* my translations of this name must be
taken purely as guesses. I am not sure that the first
element is not Creek *ikàna,* which sometimes appears in
compounds as *kàn*—compare *kànchati,* "red ground";
nor am I sure, either, that the whole name may not
have arisen through a misapprehension of *pàkanaho,*
the Creek term for the wild plum *(Prunus).* Compare
Nadube for *Danube* in the speech of French children.

KISSIMMEE. 1. A lake in Osceola County. 2. A river
of the same name, flowing from the lake southward into
Lake Okeechobee. The name of the river is spelled
Kissimmee on the Taylor War Map, 1839, as well as on
the Mackay Blake Map, 1840. 3. A town of 3,163
inhabitants, the capital of Osceola County, situated on
the Atlantic Coast Line, at the head of Lake Tohopekaliga. Cf. Norton, *op. cit.,* pp. 279-280.

The origin of *Kissimmee* is apparently unknown. If
the name is Seminole, it may begin with Sem.-Cr. *ki,*
"mulberry," or "mulberries," an assumption that is
highly dubious and leaves the rest of the word unsolved.
Nevertheless, Sem.-Cr. *àsimà,* "over there," "yonder,"
may be the second element.

MATECUMBE. 1. Lower Matecumbe Key and Upper
Matecumbe Key, links in the chain of Florida Keys, in
Monroe County, off the southern coast. 2. Matacumbe,
a place-name on Upper Matecumbe Key.

The spellings are those of the Sectional Map of Florida, Department of Agriculture, 1930. The Rand Mc-
Nally Map, 1931, gives *Matecumbe* for the Keys and
Metacumbe for the place-name on the Upper Key.
Velasco, in his *Geografía de las Indias* (1571-1574), describes the island of Metacumbe, situated at the northern
extremity of Martyr Islands;[47] Alfredo Zayas, in his
Lexicografía Antillana, p. 382, defines Matacumbe as
"rocks (keys) dangerous to navigation which in 1662
wrecked a vessel bearing gold and silver to Spain";

---

[47] Cited by Lowery, *op. cit.,* 2: 440.

Romans, in his *Florida* (1775), Appendix, xxxiv, refers to Old Matacombe. Brinton, in his *Florida Peninsula,* p. 114, expresses the opinion that *Matecumbe* is
identical with *Guaragunve,* or *Guaragumbe,* which Fontanedo described in 1575 as the largest Indian village
on Las Martires, and which he translated by *Pueblo
de Llanto,* "town of weeping."

This identification impresses me as being highly
doubtful. *-Gumbe,* indeed, may well be the same as
Spanish *-cumbe,* whereas *Guara-* can with difficulty be
regarded as an orthographic variant of Spanish *mata.*
Be that as it may, the meaning of *Matacumbe* is not
clear, though Swanton takes *Guaragunve,* with much
hesitation, for a cognate of Choctaw *wilanli,* "to weep,"
and *kowi* or *kōwi,* "desert."[48]

OCALA. A city of 7,281 inhabitants, on the Atlantic Coast
Line and the Seaboard Air Line, in Marion County.
Ocala Junction is near the city, on the Atlantic Coast
Line.

Ocala was an ancient Timucua town and province,
through which De Soto passed in 1539. The town was
near the site of the present Ocala.

Among early writers there are numerous variants of
the name: *Ocale, Ocali, Ocaly, Cale, Etocale, Olagale,
Eloquale.*

Ocala cannot be translated; it has nothing to do with
Sem.-Cr. *okholati,* "blue."

PICOLATA. A steamboat landing on the left bank of the
St. Johns River, about forty-one miles above Jacksonville. The Spaniards built a fort here in order to pro-
tect the old De Soto Trail, which crossed the river at this
point. On the right bank, across from Picolata, they
built another fort, which they called *St. Francis de Pupa.*

The sites of these forts are clearly shown, west of
St. Augustine, on the Robin-Poirson *Carte des Deux
Florides et de la Louisiane* (1807). *Picolata* also appears
on M. Bonne's *Carte de la Louisiane et de la Floride*
(1750) and on the Arrowsmith map of 1814.

In 1740 Governor Oglethorpe of Georgia, in the interest of England, captured the fort at Picolata, but

---

[48] Swanton, *BAE,* Bul. 73: 29.

failed in his efforts to take St. Augustine. The fort at Picolata has long since disappeared. Bartram, however, gives a description of its ruins as he found them in 1791.[49]

Though Picolata is the site of an ancient Indian settlement, probably Seminole, the name impresses me as being of Spanish origin. It is simply a corruption of Spanish *pico* plus *lato*, "broad bluff," the term having reference to the ground on which the fort was situated. Similar names are common along the St. Johns, such as *St. Johns Bluff, Floral Bluff, Buffalo Bluff, Bluffton,* and *Crows Bluff.*

In 1823 Vignoles expressly affirms that the ruins of the old blockhouse of Picolata, standing on a low bluff, remind the visitor of the deserted castle of some ancient feudal lord.[50]

I do not think that the first element in *Picolata* has anything to do with Creek *opiki*, "twisted."

SAMPALA. A lake in Madison County.

        1839. L. SAMPALA. Taylor Map.

        1856. L. SAMPALA. Davis Map.

A geographic name of the same form is given by Norton, *op. cit.*, p. 390.

Sampala was a former Seminole town (1823), situated above the forks of the Apalachicola River, in Calhoun County—far to the west of the Madison County name.

Sampala may be connected with Sem. *sàmpà*, "basket"; but this etymology seems to me to be very uncertain.

SUWANNEE RIVER. 1. A river which rises in Georgia, west of the Okefenokee Swamp, enters Florida near Blounts Ferry, in Hamilton County, and flowing southwestward falls into the Gulf about fifteen miles north of Cedar Key.

        1839. SUWANEE RIVER. Taylor Map.

    2. Suwannee Bay, at the mouth of the river.

        1930. SUWANNEE BAY. Sectional Map.

---

[49] William Bartram, *op. cit.*, p. 78.

[50] Quoted by William W. Dewhurst, *History of St. Augustine* (New York, 1885), p. 91.

3. A county formed in 1858, with a present population of 15,731.   4. A town of 376 inhabitants, on the Atlantic Coast Line, in Suwannee County.   5. Suwannee Valley, a hamlet on the Georgia Southern and Florida Railroad, in Columbia County—formerly called *Suwannee Shoals* (1870, 1892).

Suwannee was a former Seminole settlement which occupied the present site of Old Town, on the west bank of the Suwannee River, in Dixie County. This Seminole town was destroyed in the war of 1818. Some early spellings of the name are *Old Suwany Town* (1822), *Suahnee* (1836), *Suanee Old Town* (1836).

Suwannee, according to Brinton, is a corruption of Spanish *San Juan*, a name which, preceded by *Little*, distinguished this river from the larger St. Johns— el Rio de San Juan—on the eastern coast. Brinton gives other spellings of the name as *Little St. Johns, Little Savanna, Sequano, Suannee, Swannee.*[51]

Plausible as this derivation seems, it is nevertheless rendered highly dubious by the existence of the village Suwanee, in Gwinnett County, Georgia, which occupies the site of a former Cherokee settlement named *Suwani*. But the Cherokees believe the name *Suwani* to be of Creek origin.[52]

I am myself of the opinion that the Creeks named the Florida river, and that the corruption of the later Spanish *St. Juan* to *St. Whan* resulted in a formal confusion which is directly responsible for the Brinton etymology. The name *Suwannee*, however, cannot be translated with certainty, the lack of historical data rendering futile all guesses at its etymology. Gannett, *Geol. Bul.* 258: 294, suggests Creek *sawani*, "echo," but this interpretation, like all others, is no doubt purely fanciful.

TUSCAWILLA.   1. A station on the Jacksonville, Gainesville and Gulf Railroad, near Micanopy, in Alachua County.   2. Tuscawilla Cut, *mail* Orange Springs, in Marion County: recorded by Rand McNally, 1931.

The Taylor War Map, 1839, shows a *Tuscawilla Hk.* (Hammock) near the present Micanopy. According to Sprague, *Florida War*, p. 281, Tuscowilla Hammock covered an area of six by eighteen miles. Tuscawilla, how-

---

[51] Brinton, *op. cit.*, page 143 and footnote 3.
[52] James Mooney, in *BAE*, Rep. 19, pt. 1: 383, 532.

ever, first became known as one of the former Chickasaw towns in northwest Mississippi. Some early spellings of this name are *Tascaouilo,* 1702, *Tuskawillao,* 1720, *Taskaouilo,* 1737, and *Tascaoullou,* 1755.[53] The latest form apparently signifies "beloved warrior"—from Choctaw or Chickasaw *tàshka,* "warrior," and *hullo,* "beloved," whereas the other forms may point to Choctaw or Chickasaw *tàshka,* "warrior," and *weli,* "plunderer"—"warrior-plunderer."

UCETA. A village of fifty inhabitants, on the Atlantic Coast Line, in Hillsborough County: recorded on the Sectional Map, 1930.

On Friday, May 30, 1539, De Soto with his army landed in Florida at the head of the present Hillsborough Bay, two leagues from the town of a Timucua Indian chief named *Ucita,* otherwise *Ocita* or *Ecita.*[54]

The meaning of *Uceta* is unknown.

WACISSA. 1. A river in Jefferson County.

      1839. WACISSA R. Taylor Map.

      1856. WACISSA R. Davis Map.

2. A town with a population of 1,757, on the Seaboard Air Line, in the same county.

      1892. WACISSA. Norton, *op. cit.,* p. 42.

Wacissa is a name of Timucuan origin; its meaning is unknown. From this source has evidently sprung another name—*Owasissas*—which designated a former Seminole settlement on a branch of the St. Marks River. Its population was estimated at one hundred in 1822.

WANNEE. A station on the Seaboard Air Line, in Gilchrist County. This name, as shown on the Colton Map, 1870, was originally *Suwannee, q. v., supra.*

WAUCHULA. A town with a population of 2,574, on the Atlantic Coast Line, in Hardee County.

This name is not recorded either on the Taylor War Map of 1839 or on the Davis Map of 1856. *Wauchula* is mentioned, however, by Norton, *op. cit.,* p. 391.

---

[53] Cf. Swanton, *BAE,* Rep. 44: 212.

[54] Ranjel, in *Narratives of De Soto,* 1: 22; *ibid.,* 2: 52, 58.

Cushman takes *Wauchula* to be Choctaw, and translates the name by "many foxes," assuming *wau-* to be a mistake for *laua*, "many," and the second element to be Choctaw *chula*, "fox."[55]

This translation is certainly erroneous, because the adjective almost always follows the noun in Choctaw, exceptions to this rule being apparent rather than real. The same position of the adjective generally holds good in the Creek dialect; hence the element *chula*, whether it be Sem.-Cr. *chula*, "fox," or *chuli*, "pine tree," excludes the syllable *wau-* from connection with any adjective whatsoever. After careful study of the name, I have reached the conclusion that the second element of *Wauchula* may be the Creek adjective *achuli*, "old," "stale," as found, for instance, in *waka-culi*, "an old bull or steer"; and that the first element is possibly an abbreviation of Creek *wiwa*, "water," so that the original meaning must have been "old or stagnant water." *Wauchula*, in fact, is near Peace Creek and other streams. It may be recalled here that *Noxubee*, the name of a river and of a county in Mississippi, is a derivative of Choctaw *nakshobi*, "stinking."

As *Wauchula* is an obscure name, I will suggest one or two more sources. Perhaps *Wauchula* represents, first, an illiterate pronunciation of Sem.-Cr. *watula*, "sandhill crane" (*Grus mexicana* Müll.), just as, for instance, *chune* may replace *tune* in vulgar speech. Or if *Wauchula*, in the next place, is of Choctaw origin, the name may be a corruption of *woshulli* or *wushulli*, "to form a froth on the surface," "to ferment."

I must admit, finally, that my translations of *Wauchula* are not based on sufficient data to be considered authoritative.

WEST TOCOI. A station on the Atlantic Coast Line, in St. Johns County. The application of this name is modern; but the original *Tocoi* was a Timucua town situated at some distance from St. Augustine. The name cannot be translated.

---

[55] H. B. Cushman, *History of the Choctaw, Chickasaw, and Natchez Indians* (Austin, Texas, 1899), p. 606.

3. IMPORTED NAMES

CASSADAGA. A village with eighty-three inhabitants in Volusia County. *Cassadaga* is the name of a lake, a creek, and a village in Chautauqua County, New York. The name is said to be derived from Iroquois *gusdago*, "under the rocks."[56]

CATAWBA. A village of fifty-seven inhabitants, in Santa Rosa County. *Catawba* designates an important Siouan tribe, formerly residing on the Catawba River, in South Carolina. As late as 1728 this tribe occupied six villages on the river, scattered over a distance of twenty miles.

The probable derivation is Choctaw *katapa*, "a division," "divided," "separated."

CHICORA. A station on the Seaboard Air Line, in Polk County.

1899. CHICORA. Century Atlas.

Chicora was a name conferred on the coast of South Carolina and the Indians of that region at the time of Ayllon's visit in 1521.

The name may be derived from Catawba *Yuchi-kere*, "Yuchi are there."[57]

CONASAUGA. A station on the Atlantic Coast Line, in Manatee County.

Conasauga is the name of a river in northwestern Georgia and of a village in Polk County, Tennessee. It is a recent importation to Florida.

Conasauga is derived from Cherokee *Gansagi* or *Gansagigi*, the name of several former Cherokee settlements. The name *Canasagua* is met with as early as 1540 in the *Narratives of De Soto*. "He left Guaxule," says the Gentleman of Elvas, referring to De Soto, "and after two days' travel arrived at Canasagua, where twenty men came out from the town on the road, each laden with a basket of mulberries."[58] This town was probably near the present Kenesaw Mountain, Georgia. The name cannot be translated.[59]

---

[56] Cf. W. M. Beauchamp, *Aboriginal Place-Names of New York* (Albany, 1907), p. 40.

[57] See Hodge, *op. cit.*, 1: 263.

[58] Bourne, *Narratives of De Soto*, 1: 72-73.

[59] See Mooney, *BAE*, Rep. 19, part 1: 518-519; Hodge, *op. cit.*, 1: 656.

ERIE. A station on the Seaboard Air Line, in Manatee County; recorded by Norton, *op. cit.*, p. 92.

Erie is a city, port of entry, and county seat of Erie County, Pennsylvania; the name also characterizes the southernmost of the Great Lakes, as well as the chief canal in the United States, extending from the Hudson River at Albany to Lake Erie at Buffalo.

Erie is the name of a powerful Iroquoian tribe formerly inhabiting western New York and the southern shore of Lake Erie from Genesee to the Cuyahoga River in Ohio. *Erie* is derived from Huron (Iroquoian) *yen-resh*, "it is long-tailed," the term signifying "people of the panther." To the French this tribe was known as *Nation du Chat*, " (Wild) Cat People," doubtless because the generic term for the panther and the wildcat was probably the same in Iroquois.

HAVANA. A town with a population of 1,169, on the Seaboard Air Line, in Gadsden County.

The fact that the culture of Cuban tobacco was introduced into Gadsden County as early as 1829 is no doubt connected with the choice of the famous Cuban city as a place-name.

The etymology of *Havana*, the name of the city founded in 1515 on the southern coast of Cuba by Diego Velasquez and removed in 1579 to its present site, has not been determined. The word, however, is undoubtedly of Indian origin, though its exact signification has been lost.[60]

HIWASSEE. A village in the western part of Orange County: recorded as *Hiawassee* by Norton, *op. cit.*, p. 68.

Hiwassee was the name of several extinct Cherokee settlements. The most important of these was situated at Savannah Ford, above Columbia, Polk County, Tennessee. Note the present river-name, *Hiwassee*, in the southeastern part of Tennessee. The source of this name is Cherokee *ayuhwasi*, "meadow."

IMMOKALEE. A town with a population of 380, on the Atlantic Coast Line, in Collier County: recorded on the map in Winter's *Florida* (1918).

---

[60] J. J. Egli, *Nomina Geographica*[2] (Leipzig, 1893), p. 395.

Amakalli was a Lower Creek town, with a population of sixty men in 1799, on a creek of the same name in Georgia.

Immokalee is derived from Cherokee *ama*, "water," and *kalola*, "tumbling."

KALAMAZOO. A station on the Florida East Coast Railway, *mail* Osteen, in Volusia County.

Kalamazoo, the designation of a city in Michigan after which the Florida railroad station presumably was named, is a derivation of Old Ojibway *kikalamozo*, "he is inconvenienced by smoke in his lodge." This Ojibway source is composed of *kik*, "to be stupified," etc., and *alamozo*, a term referring to the effect of smoke, the final syllable *-zo* having special reference to the action of fire. The usual translation, "otter's tail," is false.[61]

KEUKA. A hamlet with a population of thirty-one, on the Atlantic Coast Line, in Putnam County; the name is found in Norton's *Handbook*, p. 81.

Keuka designates a lake in Yates County, New York. The name seems to be a derivative of Seneca (Iroquoian) *gwaugweh*, "taking canoes out," or "portage."[62]

Keuka is thought to be identical with *Cayuga*, a geographic name in New York that has become popular in other states.

KOMOKO. A station on the Atlantic Coast Line, in Alachua County. *Komoka* was the name of an Indian chief who lived in Michigan, according to information given me by Mr. W. E. Cummer, of the Cummer-Diggins Company, Cadillac, Michigan. When the Cummer Lumber Company established itself in Florida, it named one of its stations after this Indian, spelling his name incorrectly with a final *o*.

In Middlesex County, Canada, there is a place by the name of *Komoka*, an Indian name said to signify "young grandmother," or "owls' roost."[63]

---

[61] See W. R. Gerard, *Amer. Anthropologist*, n. s., 13 (1911) : 337-338.

[62] See W. M. Beauchamp, *Aboriginal Place-Names of New York*, pp. 133, 358; G. H. Armstrong, *The Origin and Meaning of Place-Names in Canada* (Toronto, 1930), p. 60.

[63] W. F. Moore, *Indian Place-Names in the Province of Ontario* (Toronto, 1930), p. 30.

MANATEE. 1. A river which, like the Little Manatee, empties into Tampa Bay.

1839. MANATEE RIVER. Taylor Map.

2. A county created in 1855. 3. A town of 3,129 inhabitants, on the Seaboard Air Line, in Manatee County.

1899. MANATEE. Norton, p. 59.

Manatee came into English as early as 1555 from Spanish *manati,* "sea-cow" (*Manatus americanus* or *australis.*), which has sprung in turn from the Carib languages of the mainland. In these languages the word designates the female breast, a feature characteristic of the sea-cow. The derivation from *manattoui,* "sea-cow," a Carib word of the West Indies, is inaccurate.[64]

MANDALAY. A station on the Live Oak, Perry and Gulf Railway, in the southwestern part of Taylor County.

Mandalay is a city and a district in Burma, India. The name is said to be shortened from Sanskrit *Gharamandala,* "District or Circle of Forts."[65] The use of *Mandalay* as a Florida place-name may have been inspired by the popularity of a song based on a well-known poem of Kipling's.

MANHATTAN. 1. A hamlet with one hundred inhabitants in Manatee County. 2. Manhattan Beach, on the Florida East Coast Railroad, in Duval County; see Winter, *op. cit.,* p. 168. 3. A settlement, *mail* Astor, in Lake County.

Manhattan is a borough of New York City comprising Manhattan Island, Governor's, Bidlow's, Ellis, Blackwell's, Randall's, Ward's, and Oyster Islands: area 22 square miles. The original city of New York was built on Manhattan Island. Manhattan Beach is a seaside resort on Coney Island, Kings County, New York.

Manhattan has proved to be a popular place-name, being found not only in Florida, but also in Illinois, Indiana, Kansas, Montana, Pennsylvania, and Wyoming. The name is derived from the Algonquian *manah,* "island," and *atin,* "hill"—"hill island," or "island of hills." The name originally designated a tribe of the Wappinger Confederacy that occupied Manhattan Island and its vicinity.

[64] See G. Friederici, *Hilfswörterbuch für den Amerikanisten* (Halle, 1926), p. 59.
[65] J. J. Egli, *op. cit.,* p. 351.

MATOAKA. A station on the Atlantic Coast Line, in Manatee County, *mail* Sarasota.

 1930. MATOAKA. Sectional Map.

 The real name of Pocahontas, Powhatan's daughter (1595-1617), was *Matoaka* (*Matowaka*), which Gerard derives from Algonquian *metawake,* she amuses herself playing with something."[66]

MINNEHAHA. A small lake lying south of Lake Apopka, in Lake County.

 1899. L. MINNEHAHA. Norton, *op. cit.,* p. 46.

 Minnehaha, the name of the heroine in Longfellow's *Song of Hiawatha,* is first used in Mrs. Mary Eastman's *Life and Legends of the Sioux* (New York, 1849). The source of the heroine's name has been found in Mrs. Eastman's assertion that the Indians designate by *Minnehaha,* "laughing waters," the Little Falls situated between Fort Snelling and Falls of St. Anthony. The name is usually derived from Teton (Dakota) *mini,* "water," and *haha,* "laughter"—literally "water laughter." More probably, however, it is the Dakota *mini,* "water," and *haha,* "cataract"—hence "waterfall."

MINNEOLA. 1. A village with a population of 185, on the Atlantic Coast Line and the Tavares and Gulf Railway, in Lake County. 2. A lake, also called *Cowhouse Lake,* near the village, in Lake County.

 There is a *Mineola* in each of the following States: Georgia, Iowa, Missouri, New York, North Carolina, and Texas. Furthermore, the name appears with the spelling *Minneola* in Minnesota, Kansas, and Florida.

 In the Dakota dialect *mini* signifies "water," and *ota* signifies "much"; hence the place-name *Minneota,* in Jackson County, Minnesota, is probably derived from these Dakota words, as in Warren Upham's *Minnesota Geographic Names,* p. 262. But as the Dakota (Sioux) dialect has no *l,* I do not see how *Minneola,* a place-name in Goodhue County, Minnesota, can be rendered by Upham, *ibid.,* p. 207, in the same way.

 I strongly suspect that *Mineola* (*Minneola*) is an artificial compound of the Indian *mini* with the popular termination *-ola,* after the manner of *Indianola, Cyprola,* and similar modern coinages.

---

[66] Hodge, *op. cit.,* 2: 269.

MOHAWK. A hamlet of forty-five inhabitants on the Atlantic Coast Line, in Lake County. The Mohawk tribe, an important member of the Iroquois Confederation, formerly occupied the valley of Mohawk River, in the state of New York; but since the Revolutionary War most of the tribe have resided in Canada. At least seven states, besides Florida and New York, use *Mohawk* as a geographic name; and there is also a *Mohawk* in Ontario, Canada.

Mohawk corresponds to Narragansett *Mohowauck*, "they eat (animate) things"—hence "cannibals."

MUSCOGEE. 1. A village of 295 inhabitants, on the St. Louis-San Francisco Railroad, in Liberty County: recorded by *The Century Atlas*, 1899.

The term *Muskhogean* designates a large family of tribes in the southeastern United States, comprising the Alabama, Choctaw, Hitchiti, and other linguistic branches or groups. The name *Muskogee* or *Muscogee*, from which the adjective *Muskhogean* was formed, was applied to the dominant people and language of the Creek Confederacy, which formed the largest division of the Muskhogean family. The name *Creeks*, which was conferred on the Confederacy by the English, is probably shortened from "Ocheese Creek Indians," *Ocheese* being the name of a stream on which most of the so-called Lower Creeks at one time were living.[67] *Ocheese Creek* was formerly the name of the upper part of Ocmulgee River, Georgia.[68]

The name *Muscogee* is apparently of Algonquian origin. Compare Cree *muskeg*, "swamp," *muskagoo*, "swamp Indian"; Ojibway *maskig*, "swamp," and Shawnee *muskiegui*, "lake," "pond."

NEOGA. A station on the Florida East Coast Railroad, in Flagler County.

In Cumberland County, Illinois, there is a town of about 992 inhabitants called *Neoga*, which Gannett, in *U. S. Geol. Survey*, Bul. 258, p. 221, renders by "place of the deity," without giving a specific source. This translation is wrong. The name, which was originally selected for a railroad station on the site of the present town, is slightly corrupted from *naoge*, "deer," the designation of a Seneca clan of the Iroquois Confederation.

---

[67] V. K. Crane, in *Mississippi Valley Historical Review*, 5: 339.
[68] Swanton, *BAE*, Bul. 73: 220.

NOKOMIS. A hamlet with seventy-nine inhabitants, on the Seaboard Air Line, in Sarasota County. The name is of recent application.

In Montgomery County, Illinois, there is a town by the name of *Nokomis*, with a population of 2,454.

Nokomis is the mother of Wenonah, in Longfellow's *Hiawatha.* Ojibway *nokomis* signifies "my grandmother." In Menomini legend this is the name of the grandmother of mankind and of Manabush, the Menomini hero-god.[69]

OCOEE. A town of 794 inhabitants, on the Atlantic Coast Line and Tavares and Gulf Railroad, in Orange County.

1892. OCOEE. Norton, *op. cit.*, p. 68.

Ocoee was a former Cherokee settlement on Ocoee River, near the site of the present Ocoee, Polk County, Tennessee.

Ocoee is derived from Cherokee *Uwagahi*, "apricot-vine place."

ONECO. A town with a population of 1,428, on the Atlantic Coast Line and the Seaboard Air Line, in Manatee County. The name is given by Norton, *op. cit.*, p. 388.

Oneco is a village (population 268) in Windham County, Connecticut, which was named after Oneka (c. 1640-1710), the eldest son of Uncas, a Mohegan sachem. *Oneka* was also called *Owanecco.*

The meaning of *Oneco* is uncertain; but the name may be connected with Algonquian *onike*, "to make a portage." Compare Micmac *unegun*, "portage." Whether the Florida name reproduces that in Connecticut, I do not know.

PANAMA CITY. 1. A town with a population of 5,402, on the Atlanta and St. Andrews Bay Railroad, in Bay County: recorded by Winter, Map, *op. cit.*, 1918. 2. Panama Park, a station on the Seaboard Air Line, *mail* Jacksonville, in Duval County: mentioned by Norton, p. 388.

Panama, the popular South American place-name, is of dubious origin, but probably is an Indian word having something to do with "fish."[70]

---

[69] W. J. Hoffman, in *BAE*, Rep. 14, pt. 1: 307.

[70] See Egli, *op. cit.*, pp. 689-690; Rudolf Schuller, in *International Jr. of American Linguistics*, 4: 220-223.

PETALUMA. A station on the Seaboard Air Line, in Dade County, southwest of Miami: recorded on the Sectional Map, 1930.

This is a California name, a derivative of Coast Miwok *Petaluma*, signifying "flat rock."[71] The town of Petaluma, in Sonoma County, California, has a population of 8,238.

SAMOSET. A town of eight hundred inhabitants in Manatee County, situated just north of Oneco.

1931. SAMOSET. Rand McNally Map.

Samoset was an Algonquian chief who owned the present site of the town of Bristol, Maine. His death took place probably soon after 1653. His name is possibly a derivative of Algonquian *Osamoset*, "he who walks over much."[72]

SHASTA. A station on the Atlantic Coast Line, in Levy County: recorded by Rand McNally, 1931.

The origin of *Shasta*, a name that has become popular in the geographic nomenclature of California, is obscure. According to C. H. Merriam, in the *Journal of the Washington Academy of Sciences*, 16: 522-525, *Shasta* is a Klamath name of an Indian tribe. The name is spelled in other ways: *Saste, Shasty,* and *Shastika.* Cf. also A. L. Kroeber, *BAE*, Bul. 78: 285 ff.

SECOTAN. A station on the Atlantic Coast Line, *mail* Perry, in Taylor County: recorded by Rand McNally, 1931.

An Algonquian tribe of this name occupied in 1584 the area now included in the counties of Washington, Tyrrell, Dare, Beaufort, and Hyde, North Carolina.

The name *Secotan*, which is of Algonquian origin, may signify "burnt place."

SENECA. A station on the Seaboard Air Line, in Broward County. I have not learned who selected this name; it is recorded by *The Century Atlas*, 1899.

Many places in the United States bear the name *Seneca*, some taking it ultimately from that of the celebrated Roman Stoic, Lucius Annaeus Seneca, the instructor of Nero, others reviving with this name the memory of an important Iroquoian tribe, which resided

[71] See A. L. Kroeber, *BAE*, Bul. 78: 896.
[72] For details of Samoset's career, see Hodge, *op. cit.*, 2: 421-422.

originally between Seneca Lake and Geneva River, in Western New York. Occasionally, as in the case of Seneca, Grant County, Oregon, the name is bestowed in honor of some well-known person.[73]

A former Cherokee settlement, in Oconee County, South Carolina, was corrupted from Cherokee *Isunigu* to *Seneca.* The meaning of the name is lost.

The aboriginal name *Seneca* is derived from the Dutch plural *Sennecas,* as found on maps of the early seventeenth century, a name which rests in turn on Mohegan *a'sinni,* "rock," and *-ika* or *-iga,* "place of."[74]

SIWASHE. A station on the Florida East Coast Line, in the northern part of Brevard County.

1930. SIWASHE. Sectional Map.

Siwashe is a Chinook Jargon word signifying "Indian," with particular reference to a native of the northern Pacific coast of North America. *Siwash* is a corruption of French *sauvage,* "savage," "wild." The form *Siwash* is recorded from 1852.[75] If *Siwashe* is by chance not an importation, it may be derived, like *Sowasha,* Mississippi, from Choctaw *shaui,* "raccoons," and *asha,* "are there."

Webster's derivation of *Siwash* from S*alish* is incorrect.

SUMATRA. 1. A village with a population of 625, on the Apalachicola Northern, in Liberty County.

1918. SUMATRA. Map in Winter's *Florida.*

The name *Sumatra,* which belongs to the second largest island of the Malay Peninsula, is of dubious origin. *Sumatra* has been traced by some authorities to Sanskrit *samantara,* which signifies an island "situated between two" seas, the phrase referring to the Indian Ocean and the Strait of Malacca; by other authorities to Sanskrit *samudra,* "sea," and *dipa,* "island"—that is, "island of the sea." The most plausible source, however, is Sanskrit *sumatra,* "excellent," "good," etc., a name conferred on the island when Buddhism was introduced to its inhabitants.[76]

---

[73] Cf. Lewis A. McArthur, *Oregon Geographic Names,* p. 315.

[74] Cf. Louise Welles Murray, *Selected Manuscripts of General John S. Clark,* etc., p. 24; Hodge, *op. cit.,* 2: 504.

[75] R. H. Thornton, *An American Glossary,* 2: 800.

[76] See *Sumatra,* in *Enciclopedia Universal Ilustrada,* 58: 830; and J. J. Egli, *op. cit.,* p. 889.

TACOMA. A station on the Atlantic Coast Line and the Jacksonville, Gainesville and Gulf Railroad, in Alachua County.

Tacoma, the principal city of Pierce County, Washington, is situated on Tacoma Harbor. The origin and meaning of *Tacoma* are not clear.

TORONTO. A station on the Atlantic Coast Line, in Orange County.

1930. TORONTO. Sectional Map.

The origin of *Toronto*, the name of the capital of the province of Ontario, Canada, remains uncertain in spite of many efforts at a satisfactory solution.[77]

UMATILLA. 1. A town of 907 inhabitants, on the Atlantic Coast Line, in Lake County.

1892. UMATILLA. Norton, *op. cit.*, p. 46.

Umatilla originally designated a river in Oregon. As the name of a Shahaptian tribe formerly inhabiting the banks of this river and the adjacent stretches of the Columbia River, *Umatilla* is not very old. *Umatilla* is also the name of a county and a town in Oregon, as well as of a waterfall in Washington.

Umatilla may mean "water rippling over sand."[78]

WABASSO. A village of three hundred inhabitants, on the Florida East Coast Railroad, in Indian River County: recorded on the Sectional Map, 1930.

Though I have not been able to get any reliable information about *Wabasso*, I take the name to be a reversal of *Ossabaw*; a designation of an island and a sound situated off the coast of Georgia, just south of Savannah. *Ossabaw* is the English form of an ancient Guale town, which appears in the Spanish of Ibarra as *Asopo*. The Guale Indian tribe, or tribes, inhabited the Atlantic Coast from Savannah River, Georgia, as far south as St. Andrews Sound. The language that they spoke was Muskhogean, but I doubt whether *Asopo* or *Ossabaw* can now be translated with any degree of certainty.[79]

[77] Cf. Eugéne Rouillard, *Noms Géographiques de la Province de Québec*, etc. (Quebec, 1906), p. 97.

[78] See Lewis A. McArthur, *Oregon Geographic Names*, p. 364.

[79] See Swanton, *BAE*, Bul. 73: 15, 80 ff.

WAUSAU.   A town of 949 inhabitants, situated on the
Alabama and West Florida Railroad, in Washington
County: recorded by *The Century Atlas,* 1899.

Two more places bear this name: the one is the
county seat of Marathon County, Wisconsin, and the
other—spelled *Wausa*—is a town in Knox County,
Nebraska.

The Menomini Indians say that an Ojibway was once
asked where he was going and answered, *"wasa, wasa,"*
"far, far." This answer is responsible for the name of
the town.

Wausau is derived from Ojibway or Menomini *wasa,*
"far," "distant."[80]

YUKON.   A hamlet of sixty-one inhabitants on the Atlantic
Coast Line, in Duval County.   This is strictly a modern
importation.

Yukon, the name of a river and a territory of Northwest Canada, signifies "the river," in an Athapascan dialect.   The name is said to have been first applied to the
river by J. Bell of the Hudson Bay Company, in 1847.
The name originally designated that part of the stream
which lies below Tanana.   The Eskimo call the Yukon
kvikhpak, "large river."[81]

---

[80] See W. J. Hoffman, in *BAE,* Rep. 14, pt. 1: 327-328.

[81] Cf. G. H. Armstrong, *op. cit.,* p. 311; and A. Hrdlicka, in *BAE,* Rep. 46:
126 ff.

4. SUNDRY NAMES ON TAYLOR'S WAR MAP

The Indian place-names of the Taylor War Map have almost all been included in the present study. It may now be proper to attempt translations of the rest.

ARTA HATCHEE. A stream in what is now Okeechobee County. As there is no *r* in Seminole, Creek, Hitchiti, and Choctaw, *Arta* is probably a corruption of Creek *oto,* "chestnut," or Creek *àta,* "lizzard." *Hatchee* is, of course, Creek *hàchi,* "creek."

The chestnut tree now grows in the counties of Okaloosa, Dade, and Hendry; it may formerly have been found in other parts of Florida, according to my colleagues, Professors C. F. Moreland and C. A. Brown.

In the De Soto narratives of 1540 reference is made to Athahachi or Atahachi, an Indian village that was situated six miles northeast of the present town of Marion, in Perry County, Alabama.[82] I take *Athahachi* to be identical in meaning with the Florida name.

The following paragraph is taken from Ranjel's account of the meeting of De Soto and the chief of Athahachi:

"Sunday, October 10, the Governor entered the village of Tascaluca, which is called Athahachi, a recent village. And the chief was on a kind of balcony on a mound at one side of the square, his head covered by a kind of coif like the almaizal, so that his headdress was like a Moor's which gave him an aspect of authority; he also wore a *pelote* or mantle of feathers down to his feat, very imposing; he was seated on some high cushions, and many of the principal men among his Indians were with him. He was as tall as that Tony of the Emperor, our lord's guard, and well proportioned, a fine and comely figure of a man. He had a son, a young man as tall as himself but more slender. Before this chief there stood always an Indian of graceful mien holding a parasol on a handle something like a round and very large fly fan, with a cross similar to that of the Knights of the Order of St. John of Rhodes, in the middle of a black

---

[82] Cf. *Handbook of the Alabama Anthropological Society* (Montgomery, Ala., 1920), p. 43.

field, and the cross was white. And although the Governor entered the plaza and alighted from his horse and went up to him, he did not rise, but remained passive in perfect composure and as if he had been a king."[83]

CHICKASAW HATCHEE. A stream that falls into the St. Johns River, near Lake Poinsett, in the southeastern corner of Orange County. This name is no longer used.

Chickasaw, the name of a powerful Muskhogean tribe, cannot be translated. *Hatchee* is Creek *hàchi*, "creek," "river."

CHITTO HATCHEE. A stream situated in what is now Okeechobee County.

The name is composed of Sem.-Cr. *chito*, "snake," and *hàchi*, "creek." This name is obsolete.

E-TO-TOE-WAL-KEE. A tributary of the St. Johns, in what is now Brevard County.

This name, now obsolete, is derived from Sem.-Cr. *ito*, "tree," and *tolki*, "fallen"—"creek of the fallen tree."

HATCHEE LUSTEE CREEK. A stream situated west of Lake Tohopekaliga.

The name means "black creek," the source being Sem.-Cr. *hàchi*, "creek," and *làsti*, "black."

OCITLOTA FUNKA. A stream now called *Spring Warrior*, in Taylor County.

It is difficult to interpret the first part of this name. In Sprague's *Florida War*, p. 434, the name is spelled *Sho-elota Funka*. Little significance can be attached to the use of the hyphen in *Sho-elota;* otherwise the name might be regarded as a derivative of Sem.-Cr. *icho*, "deer," *ili*, "tracks," and *oti*, "island," or "beach," with Sem.-Cr. *fànki*, "projecting," "jutting"—hence "jutting deer tracks beach." If we disregard the hyphen, we may derive *Shoelota* from Sem.-Cr. *choli* or *chuli*, "pine," and *oti*, "beach"—hence "jutting (*fànki*) pine tree beach."

---

[83] *Narratives of De Soto*, 2: 120-121.

There is left the remote possibility that *Sho-elota* signifies "fox den," from Sem.-Cr. *chula,* "fox," and *huti,* "den."

I can do nothing with Taylor's spelling *Ocitlota,* in which *tl* is apparently equivalent to the Sem.-Cr. voiceless *l,* and renders futile any effort to connect the first three letters, *oci-* with Sem.-Cr. *ochi,* "hickory."

OKAWILLA SAVANNA. A prairie lying south of Big Santa Fe Pond, now Santa Fe Lake, in Alachua County.

I believe *Okawilla* to be of Choctaw origin. *Lochloosa,* the name of a lake situated southwest of the savanna, is undoubtedly Choctaw, and so, too, is *Tuscawilla, supra. Oka* is "water," in Choctaw, whereas *willa,* in *Okawilla,* is probably shortened from Choctaw *wilaha,* "slimy."

OK-HOL-WA-KEE, or BIG CYPRESS SWAMP. A swamp lying just west of Lake Tohopekaliga.

Hitchiti *oki,* "water," with Sem.-Cr. *holwaki,* "bad," is the source of this name.

TCIANHATKEE. A geographic name just south of Lake Ahapopka, now Apopka, which lies on the western boundary of Orange County.

Tcianhatkee signifies "white cedar," the elements of the name being Sem.-Cr. *àchinà,* "cedar," and *hàtki,* "white."

The tree described in this name is the *Southern white cedar*—also called *post* or *swamp cedar*—technically known as *Chamaecyparis thyoides* (L.) B. S. P.

WEELAWNEE RIVER. A tributary of Wacissa River, in what is now Jefferson County.

This name is a derivative of Sem.-Cr. *wi-,* "water," and *lani,* "yellow"—"yellow water."

IV. NAMES OF VARIOUS INDIAN CHIEFS

On May 9, 1832, a treaty between the United States and the Seminole Nation of Indians was made at Payne's Landing, twenty-five miles down the Oklawaha River, in the territory of Florida, in accordance with which the Seminoles were to relinquish all claim to their lands in Florida, and emigrate West to the country of the Creeks, within three years after the ratification of the treaty. The Seminoles were to receive an additional extent of territory in proportion to their numbers.

The following Indians signed the treaty, according to Sprague, *op. cit.*, page 75:

Holati Emathlar	Tokose Emathla, or John
Jumper	Hicks
Fuch-ta-lus-ta-Hadjo	Cat-sha-Tustenuggee
Charley Emathla	Holat-a-Micco
Coi Hadjo	Hitch-it-i-Mico
Ar-pi-ucki, or Sam Jones	E-ne-hah
Ya-Ha-Hadjo	Ya-ha-Emathla-Chopco
Mico-noha	Moki-his-she-larni

The Seminoles became bitterly dissatisfied with the idea of leaving Florida and repudiated the terms of the treaty. They slew Charley Emathla because of his favorable attitude towards emigration; they assassinated General Thompson, who had imprisoned Osceola for five days at Fort King; and on December 28, 1835, under the leadership of Micanopy, Jumper, and Halpatter-Tustenugge, they massacred almost to a man Major F. L. Dade and his detachment of a hundred troops. This massacre marked the virtual beginning of the Seminole War of seven years.

I will now give the signification of these names, taking them in the same order as that in Sprague's work:

HOLATI EMATHLAR. This name is a compound of *holahta*, "chief," a term found in Creek, Apalachee, and Timucua; and of *imala*, a Creek war-title that may be rendered by "messenger," or "leader." Compare Gatschet, *Creek Migration Legend*, I, 163; II, 94. Sprague, however, *op. cit.*, p. 64, renders *Holata Emathla* by "Blue Warrior." If this translation were correct, the adjective would follow the noun, as in Creek *fus-okholati*, "blue bird," *pàhi-okholati*, "blue-grass."

JUMPER. Jumper, or Otee-Emathlar, was a cunning and intelligent Indian who acted as Micanopy's lawyer: see Sprague, *op. cit.*, p. 97. The Indian designation of Jumper signifies, I presume, "island leader," from Sem.-Cr. *oti,* "island," and *imala,* "leader"—unless *otee* can be connected with Sem.-Cr. *huti,* "home."

FUCH-TA-LUS-TA-HADJO. The first element in this name looks as if it might be derived from Sem.-Cr. *fucho,* "duck." I believe, indeed, that the variant *Fuch-a-lusta-hadjo,* in Sprague's volume, p. 74, cannot be interpreted otherwise than by "mad black duck," the other two elements in the name being Creek *làsti,* "black," and *hajo,* "mad." Nevertheless, the name may be corrupted from Sem.-Cr. *fus hàchi,* "bird creek," *làsti,* and *hajo.* *Fus hàchi* is extremely popular in Creek war names; so, too, is *hajo,* which is found also as a loan-word in Choctaw.

CHARLEY EMATHLA. Charley is a popular corruption of Seminole *chalo,* "trout," and *Emathla* signifies, roughly speaking, a "leader," from *imala.*

COI HADJO. The first element in this name is obscure. Norton, *op. cit.*, p. 374, renders the name of this famous chief by "mad partridge"; and as Sem.-Cr. *kowiki* signifies "partridge" (quail), this translation may be correct. On the other hand, *coi* may be either an abbreviation of Cr. *koakochi,* "wildcat," or a corruption of Cr. *koha,* "cane." I should mention here the occurrence not only of such Creek war names as *Koakodji hadjo,* "mad wildcat," and *Koha làko hadjo,* "mad big cane," but also of the Creek clan names, *Kohasakàlgi* or *Kohosàlgi,* "cane clan," and *Koakotchàlgi,* "wildcat clan."[84] Sprague, let me say in conclusion, gives the variant *Coahajo,* as the name of the Seminole chief—*op. cit.*, p. 65.

ARPIUCKI, or SAM JONES. This Indian, the chief of the Mikasuki tribe, lived for many years at Silver Spring, about five miles and a half from the present site of Ocala, where he was known as Sam Jones the fisherman. A great medicine man, he planned war parties and encouraged his band by incantations with roots, barks,

---

[84] See Swanton, *BAE,* Rep. 42: 104, 116.

snake and animal skins, and midnight songs. At the
outbreak of the war he was about seventy years old.
The signification of Sam Jones's Indian name has been
discussed, *supra*, under *Aripeka*.

YA-HA-HADJO. This name signifies "mad wolf," from
Creek *yahà*, "wolf," and *hajo*, "mad."

Mad Wolf was a member of the Indian delegation
who visited Arkansas in 1833 with a view to ascer-
taining whether the lands there would make a satisfactory new home for the Seminoles. He was also a signer
of the additional treaty with the United States, drawn
March 28, 1833, in accordance with which the Seminoles
relinquished all claim to the land they occupied in the
territory of Florida, and agreed to emigrate to the country assigned them in the West.

MICO-NOHA. This place is intended for Miconopi, one of
the well-known signers of the treaty. He was the head
of the Seminole nation, and about fifty years old at the
outbreak of the Seminole War. He was so fat and lazy
that his warriors are said to have carried him by force
to the scenes of battle. For the meaning of *Miconopi*,
see *Micanopy, supra*.

TOKOSE EMATELA, or JOHN HICKS. This name seems
to be connected with *takosa*, an abbreviation of Creek
takosàlgi, "mole clan," and *imala*, "leader." John Hicks,
a Mikasuki chief, was in favor of the emigration of the
Indians to the West, but died shortly before the outbreak of the Seminole War.

CAT-SHA-TUSTENUGGEE. This name is derived from
Creek *kachà*, "panther," and *tàstànàgi*, "warrior."

HOLAT-A-MICCO. As both *holahta* and *miko* are Creek
for "chief," this name may be rendered freely by "head
chief."

HITCH-I-TI-MICO. Two sources have been suggested for
the tribal name *Hitchiti*: first, Creek *ahichita*, "to look
up" (the stream), a name applied originally to a creek
at its junction with the Chattahoochee; and secondly,
Creek *achik-hàta*, "white heap" (of ashes). The name
signifies "Hitchiti chief."[85]

---

[85] Gatachet, *op. cit.*, 1: 77; Swanton, *BAE*, Bul. 73: 172 ff.

E-NE-HAH. Creek *hiniha,* the origin of this name, is a busk and war title signifying "lieutenant." In the Timucuan language *inihi* is the word for "consort."

YAHA-EMATHLA-CHOPCO. This name is derived from Creek *yahà,* "wolf," *imala,* "leader," and *chàpko,* "tall" —"tall wolf leader."

MOKI-HIS-SHE-LARNI. This name signifies "yellow tobacco dust," from Sem.-Cr. *moki,* "dust," *hichi,* "tobacco," and *lani,* "yellow."

Sprague, in his *Florida War,* gives the names of many other Indians who took part in the Seminole War. Here are some of these names and their meanings, together with the number of the page on which each name is mentioned in Sprague's volume:

344. **AHHA-TASTENUGGEE.** This name is derived from Cr. *aha,* "potato," and *tàstànàgi,* "warrior." Cf. *Aha-lak-Tustenuggee, supra.*

271. **ASSINAWAR.** This name signifies Spanish "moss," from Sem.-Cr. *asunwà.* Among the Creeks there seems to have been a moss clan called *Asunàlgi.*

22. **CHEFISCICO HAJO.** This name is derived from Sem.-Cr. *icho,* "deer," *fiksiko,* "heartless," and *hajo,* "mad"—"mad heartless deer."

228. **CHITTO-TUSTENUGGEE.** The source of this name is Sem.-Cr. *chito,* "snake," and *tàstànàgi,* "warrior." This man succeeded Sam Jones, or Arpeika, as the principal chief of the Seminoles in 1839.

397. **CHOLOTIKY.** This is a puzzling name. It may be derived from Cr. *choli,* "pine tree," and *tàikità,* "ford," crossing," or from Cr. *chulotka,* "cricket."

98, 271. **COACOOCHEE.** This Indian was probably the most dangerous of all the Seminole chiefs. His name is derived from Creek *koakochi,* "wildcat" (*Felis couguar* Kerr). With a band of eighty warriors he overran the country lying between St. Augustine and the head of the St. Johns River.

395. COTZAR-FIXICO-CHOPCO. This Indian is described as a desperate Mikasuki chief. His name signifies "tall heartless panther," from Cr. *kachà*, "panther," *fiksiko*, "heartless," and *chàpko*, "tall," or "long."

255. ECHO-E-MARTHLAR. This was a Tallahassee chief, who, with sixty followers, was arrested and sent West in 1841. The name of the chief is derived from Cr. *icho*, "deer," and *imala*, "messenger," etc.

22. ECONCHATIMICO. This name signifies "red ground chief." The name is Creek *ikàna*, "earth," *chati*, "red," and *miko*, "chief."

50, 76. FEE-KE-LUSTA. This Indian's name is corrupted from *faki*, "dirt," and *làsti*, "black—"black dirt." Black Dirt was a member of the party that went to inspect the lands in the West.

252. HALLECK TUSTENUGGEE. This chief was a fearless Mikasuki. His name is derived from Cr. *ahalak*, "potato," and *tàstànàgi*, "warrior."

 Hallec-Hajo, Sprague, p. 194, is another name in which the first element is taken from Cr. *ahalak. Hajo* is Creek for "mad."

97. HALPATTER-TUSTENUGGEE, or ALLIGATOR. Intelligent and crafty, he was considered one of the most dangerous foes of the United States troops. His name signifies "alligator warrior," from Sem.-Cr. *hàlpàtà*, "alligator," and *tàstànàgi*, "warrior."

178. HOETH-LEE-MA-TEE. This name is derived from Cr. *huli* or *holi*, "war," and *homahti*, "leader." This chief was one of those who signed terms of capitulation with the United States on March 6, 1837.

98. HOLARTOOCHEE. This chief, after leading his band for three years, surrendered to the forces of the United States and advised others to follow his example. His name signifies "little chief," the source being Sem.-Cr. *holahta*, "chief," and *-uchi*, "little." Sprague, *op. cit.*, p. 178, records his name as *Holatoochee* or *Davy*.

316. HOLATTER MICCO, or BILLY BOWLEGS. This Indian name has been analyzed, *supra*. Bowlegs, one of the most active war-chiefs, was subject to the mandates both of Sam Jones and of the Prophet (*Otulke Thlocko*).

91. ILLIS-HIGHER-HADJO. This was the name of a great medicine-chief, who arranged on a ten-foot pole the scalps of those slain at Dade's Massacre in 1835. The name is corrupted from Creek *hilis*, "medicine," *hili*, "good," and *hajo*, "mad"—"mad good medicine."

78. NE-HA-THO-CLO. The name of this chief is derived from Creek *hiniha*, "lieutenant," and *làko*, "big"— "big lieutenant."

99. NETHLOCKE-MATHLAR. This name is a poor spelling of Creek *hiniha*, "lieutenant," *làko*, "big," and *imala*, "leader," "assistant," or "messenger."

Nethlocke-mathla was the brother of Thlock-lo-Tustenuggee, "fish warrior," with whom he was continually disputing over the government of the Seminole town of Tallahassee.

22. NINNEE HOMATA TUSTENUKY. This name is derived from Sem.-Cr. *nini*, "road," *homahti*, "leader," and *tàstànàgi*, "warrior"—"road leader warrior."

188. NOCOSE-YOHOLO. This name signifies "bear yahola," from Cr. *nokosi*, "bear," and *yahola*, a word which has been discussed under *Osceola, supra*.

232. OCHE-HADJO. He was a brother of Blue Snake. His name is derived from Creek *ochi*, "hickory nut," and *hajo*, "mad." One of the Creek clans was called "hickory nut" (*ochiàlgi*).

505. OCTIARCHE. This Indian chief, a Creek by birth, resided with his band in the vicinity of Steinhatchie River, about eighty miles south of Tallahassee. He was one of those who lived to emigrate to Arkansas.

Octiarche seems to be connected with *oktahàchi*, "sand creek."

462. O-SON-E MICCO (The King of the Lakes). This name is derived from Cr. *osànà*, "otter," and *miko*, "chief."

270-271. OTULKE-THLOKO. This chief, an associate of Arpeika or Sam Jones, was known to the whites as the Prophet. Otulke exercised a profound influence over the minds of the other Indians, deluding them with midnight fires, dances, songs, and the use of roots as medicine. Even such intrepid chiefs as Holatter Micco (Billy Bowlegs), Assinawar, and Fuse Hadjo ("mad bird"), feared his power and remained for a long time under his domination. Otulke's home was in the Big Cypress Swamp, south of the Caloosahatchee River.

Otulka is derived from Cr. *hotàlgi*, "wind clan," and *thloko* is Cr. *làko*, "big"—"big wind-clan" chief.

On pages 396 and 397 Sprague gives *Hotulka*, a variant closer to the Indian source, as the name of an Indian chief.

472, 504. PASCOFFER. This chief was in command of the Creek Indians on the Ochlockonee River. His name signifies "dancing ground," from Creek *paskofà.*

430. POWIS-FIXICO (Short Grass). The translation given by Sprague is inaccurate. *Fixico* is the Creek *fiksiko*, "heartless," and *powis* probably results from a folk etymologist's substitution of the Welsh surname for the obscure Indian word. "Grass" is *pàhi* in Creek, whereas *powis* is Welsh for "peace." The name of this Indian appears in Sprague's volume, p. 444, as *Powis Cockuchinies [Cockuchinie's]*, a designation in which *Cockuchinies* is a corruption of Cr. *kochukni*, "short."

317. SHO-NOCK-HADJO. This was a sub-chief, whose name signifies "mad Shawnee," from Cr. *sawanok*, "Shawnee," and *hajo*, "mad."

318. SOLO MICCO. The origin of this name is Sem.-Cr. *suli*, "buzzard," and *miko*, "chief"—"buzzard chief."

97. TA-HO-LOO-CHEE, or LITTLE CLOUD. This Indian was remarkable for his hatred of the whites. The form *Ta-ho-loo-chee* is a corruption of Sem.-Cr. *aholochi*, "cloud." Sprague, *op. cit.*, p. 178, records this name as *Yaholoochee* or *Cloud*.

99, 502, 503. THLOCH-LO-TUSTENUGGEE. This name is erroneously translated by "Tigertail," which in Creek would be *kachà*, "panther," and *hàchi*, "tail." In America the panther was formerly often called a tiger.

At a ball game in which this Indian took part at Fort Moultrie, he wore the skin of a panther attached to his belt. Thereafter he was known as *Tigertail*.

Tigertail was captured in 1842, but died at the barracks in New Orleans, while he was awaiting, with 250 other Indians, transportation up the Mississippi to his future home in Arkansas.

Thlock-lo-Tustenuggee is intended for Cr. *làlo*, "fish," and *tàstànàgi*, "warrior."

22. TUSKANEHA. I take this name, though somewhat doubtfully, to be a derivative of Cr. *taski*, "sapsucker" (*Sphyrapicus varius varius* L.) and *hiniha*, "lieutenant."

A similar name, also on page 22, is *Tuski Hajo*, "mad sapsucker." If *Tuski Hajo* were of Choctaw origin, the meaning would be "mad warrior," from *tàshka*, "warrior," and *hajo* or *hacho*, "mad," a loanword from Creek.

The first element, however, in *Tuskaneha* and *Tuski Hajo* may represent Creek *tàsikaia*, "citizen."

196. TUSTENUCK-COCHO-CONEE. The source of this name is Cr. *tàstànàgi*, "warrior," and *kochokni*, "short"—"short warrior."

V. CONCLUSION

The prosaic character of the native geographic names in Florida is remarkable. Animals, fish, reptiles, trees, conspicious features of the landscape, trivial incidents, and personal names form the chief sources from which these names are drawn—drawn, with keen powers of observation, it is true, but apparently with little or no display of emotion on the part of the Indian. Among the numerous native names comprised in this study there is, indeed, scarcely a single one that would appeal to a white man's sense of beauty.

Such, too, is doubtless the character of most Indian names wherever they may be found in North America. On the other hand, I am familiar with some names, especially in Louisiana, which make a strong appeal not only to the intellect but also to the heart. *Tickfaw*, harsh as it may sound, is the designation of a beautiful little river which flows through the piny region of Louisiana; and *Tickfaw*— in the Choctaw tongue *tiakfoha*—probably signifies "pine rest," or more freely, "rest among the pines." *Chacahoula* and *Catahoula*, alike novel in form, are also Choctaw names, the former meaning "beloved home" *(chuka hullo)*, and the latter "beloved lake" *(okhàta hullo)*. Whether *Cabahannosé*, an ancient name for a Louisiana bayou, exhibits more of the Indian's fancy than his accuracy of observation, I am willing to leave to the reader's judgment; for *cabahanossé*, a derivation of Choctaw *hankhobanosi*, corresponds roughly to the English "where the wild duck sleeps." Is, then, *Cabahannosé* of necessity less poetical or romantic, say, than Scott's "The stag at eve had drunk his fill?" Or is not *peni intalaia*—to take another example from the Choctaw— strong in its emotional appeal for the very reason that it signifies literally "the boat's trail," a phrase which in plain English becomes "a ferry"?

If the imagination of the Indian has less extensive boundaries, it may, nevertheless, possess a simplicity and a subtlety which are denied to the imagination of the white man.

The imagination of the Indian is aroused, to a great extent, by that which he sees and hears; whereas the imagination of the white man is moulded, to an extent equally great or even greater, by his familiarity with much that is lovely and imperishable, enshrined in the literatures of the world and brought down to him from a thousand yesterdays.

The Indian personal names included in my study may be dismissed with a brief comment. Most of these names are obviously war or busk titles; others are taken from the geographic features of the homes of Indian chiefs; and still others, relatively few in number, are reminiscent of certain Indian clans.

LIST OF PUBLICATIONS MOST FREQUENTLY CONSULTED

Brinton, Daniel G. *Notes on the Floridian Peninsula*, etc. Philadelphia, 1859.

Bourne, Edward G. (editor). *Narratives of the Career of Hernando de Soto*. 2 Vols. New York, 1904.

Byington, Cyrus. *A Dictionary of the Choctaw Language* (Edited by John R. Swanton and Henry S. Halbert, *Bureau of American Ethnology*, Bul. 46). Washington 1915.

Gatschet, Albert S. *A Migration Legend of the Creek Indians*. Vol. I (Brinton's *Library of Aboriginal American Literature*, No. 4). Philadelphia, 1884; Vol. II *(Translations of the Academy of Science*, Vol. V, Nos. 1 and 2). St. Louis, 1888.

Hodge, Frederick W. *Handbook of American Indians (Bureau of American Ethnology*, Bul. 30), Part 1, Washington, 1907; Part 2, Washington, 1910.

Lanier, Sidney. *Florida: Its Scenery, Climate, and History*. Philadelphia, 1876.

Loughridge, R., and Hodge, David M. *Dictionary of the Muskokee or Creek Language in Creek and English*. St. Louis, 1890.

Lowery, Woodbury. *The Spanish Settlements within the Present Limits of the United States*. Vol. I (1513-1561), New York and London, 1901; Vol. II (1562-1574), New York and London, 1905.

Maps of Florida.

MacCauley, Clay. *The Seminole Indians of Florida (Bureau of American Ethnology*, Rep. 5). Washington, 1887.

Mooney, James. *Myths of the Cherokee (Bureau of American Ethnology*, Rep. 19, part 1). Washington, 1900.

Moore-Wilson, Minnie. *The Seminoles of Florida*. Philadelphia, 1896.

Norton, Charles L. *A Handbook of Florida*. With forty-nine maps and illustrations. Third edition, revised. New York, 1892.

Sprague, John T. *The Origin, Progress, and Conclusion of the Seminole War*. New York, 1848.

Swanton, John R. *Early History of the Creek Indians and Their Neighbors (Bureau of American Ethnology*, Bul. 73). Washington, 1922.

—— *Creek Social Organization and Usages*, and other papers *(Bureau of American Ethnology*, Rep. 42). Washington, 1928.

Winter, Nevin O. *Florida: The Land of Enchantment*. Boston, 1918.

INDEX OF NAMES